Elasticsearch Essentials

Harness the power of Elasticsearch to build and manage scalable search and analytics solutions with this fast-paced guide

Bharvi Dixit

BIRMINGHAM - MUMBAI

Elasticsearch Essentials

First published: January 2016

Production reference: 1250116

Published by Packt Publishing Ltd.
Livery Place
35 Livery Street
Birmingham B3 2PB, UK.

ISBN 978-1-78439-101-0

www.packtpub.com

Credits

Author
Bharvi Dixit

Reviewer
Alberto Paro

Commissioning Editor
Pramila Balan

Acquisition Editor
Sonali Vernekar

Content Development Editor
Kirti Patil

Technical Editor
Ryan Kochery

Copy Editor
Kausambhi Majumdar

Project Coordinator
Nidhi Joshi

Proofreader
Safis Editing

Indexer
Tejal Daruwale Soni

Graphics
Abhinash Sahu

Production Coordinator
Manu Joseph

Cover Work
Manu Joseph

About the Author

Bharvi Dixit is an IT professional with an extensive experience of working on the search servers (especially Elasticsearch) and NoSQL databases. He is currently working as a technology and search expert with GrownOut, a SAAS-based referral hiring solution provider company. He is the organizer and speaker of Delhi's Elasticsearch Meetup Group, which is one of the fastest growing Elasticsearch communities in India.

He also works as a freelance Elasticsearch consultant and has helped many small to medium size organizations in adapting Elasticsearch for different use cases such as, creating search solutions for big data-automated intelligence platforms in the area of counter-terrorism and risk management as well as in other domains such as recruitment, e-commerce, finance and log monitoring.

He holds a master's degree in computer science from LBSIM - Delhi, India, and has a keen interest in creating scalable backend platforms. His other interest area are data analytics, distributed computing, automations, and DevOps. Java and Python are the primary languages in which he loves to write code, and he has already built a proprietary software for consultancy firms.

In his spare time, he loves writing blogs and reading the latest technology books. He can be connected through LinkedIn at `https://in.linkedin.com/in/bharvidixit`.

Acknowledgments

I would like to thank my family for their continuous support, specially my brother, Patanjali Dixit, who always guided me at each step throughout my career. I would also like to give a big thanks to Lavleen for the support, patience, and encouragement she gave during all those days when I was busy writing this book.

I would like to extend my thanks to all of the Packt team working on this book and our technical reviewer, Alberto Paro. Without them, the book wouldn't have been as great as it is now. It was one of the best team i have worked with.

Finally, special thanks to Shay Banon for creating Elasticsearch and to all the people who contributed to the libraries and modules published around this project.

Once again, thank you.

About the Reviewer

Alberto Paro is an engineer, project manager, and software developer. He currently works as a CTO at Big Data Technologies and as a freelance international consultant on software engineering for big data and NoSQL solutions. He loves to study emerging solutions and applications mainly related to Big Data processing, NoSQL, natural language processing, and neural networks. He began programming in BASIC on a Sinclair Spectrum when he was eight years old, and he has a lot of experience of using different operating systems, applications, and programming languages.

In 2000, he graduated in computer science engineering from Politecnico di Milano with a thesis on designing multiuser and multidevice web applications. He assisted the professors at the university for about a year. Then, he came in contact with The Net Planet Company and loved their innovative ideas; he started working on knowledge management solutions and advanced data mining products. In the summer of 2014, his company was acquired by Big Data technologies, where he currently works and uses mainly Scala and Python on state-of-the-art Big Data software (Spark, Akka, Cassandra, and YARN). In 2013, he started freelancing as a consultant for Big Data technologies, machine learning, and Elasticsearch.

In his spare time, when he is not playing with his children, he likes to work on open source projects. When he was in high school, he started contributing to projects related to the GNOME environment (gtkmm). One of his preferred programming languages is Python, and he wrote one of the first NoSQL backends on Django for MongoDB (Django-MongoDB-engine). He is also a fan of the Scala language and enjoys spreading his love of technology: he was a presenter of Big Data concepts at Scala Day Italy 2015 on Scala.JS and Big Data Tech Italian Conference in Florence.

In 2010, he began using Elasticsearch to provide search capabilities to some Django e-commerce sites and developed PyES (a Pythonic client for Elasticsearch), as well as the initial part of the Elasticsearch MongoDB driver. He is the author of *ElasticSearch Cookbook* and *ElasticSearch Cookbook Second Edition* as well as a technical reviewer of *Elasticsearch Server, Second Edition*, and the video course, *Building a Search Server with ElasticSearch*, all of which have been published by *Packt Publishing*.

www.PacktPub.com

Support files, eBooks, discount offers, and more

For support files and downloads related to your book, please visit www.PacktPub.com.

Did you know that Packt offers eBook versions of every book published, with PDF and ePub files available? You can upgrade to the eBook version at www.PacktPub.com and as a print book customer, you are entitled to a discount on the eBook copy. Get in touch with us at service@packtpub.com for more details.

At www.PacktPub.com, you can also read a collection of free technical articles, sign up for a range of free newsletters and receive exclusive discounts and offers on Packt books and eBooks.

https://www2.packtpub.com/books/subscription/packtlib

Do you need instant solutions to your IT questions? PacktLib is Packt's online digital book library. Here, you can search, access, and read Packt's entire library of books.

Why subscribe?
- Fully searchable across every book published by Packt
- Copy and paste, print, and bookmark content
- On demand and accessible via a web browser

Free access for Packt account holders

If you have an account with Packt at www.PacktPub.com, you can use this to access PacktLib today and view 9 entirely free books. Simply use your login credentials for immediate access.

Table of Contents

Preface

With constantly evolving and growing datasets, organizations have the need to find actionable insights for their business. Elasticsearch, which is the world's most advanced search and analytics engine, brings the ability to make massive amounts of data usable in a matter of milliseconds. It not only gives you the power to build blazingly fast search solutions over a massive amount of data, but can also serve as a NoSQL data store.

Elasticsearch Essentials will guide you to become a competent developer quickly with a solid knowledge and understanding of the Elasticsearch core concepts. In the beginning, this book will cover the fundamental concepts required to start working with Elasticsearch and then it will take you through more advanced concepts of search techniques and data analytics.

This book provides complete coverage of working with Elasticsearch using Python and Java APIs to perform CRUD operations, aggregation-based analytics, handling document relationships, working with geospatial data, and controlling search relevancy.

In the end, you will not only learn about scaling Elasticsearch clusters in production, but also how to secure Elasticsearch clusters and take data backups using best practices.

What this book covers

Chapter 1, Getting Started with Elasticsearch, provides an introduction to Elasticsearch and how it works. After going through the basic concepts and terminologies, you will learn how to install and configure Elasticsearch and perform basic operations with Elasticsearch.

Chapter 2, Understanding Document Analysis and Creating Mappings, covers the details of the built-in analyzers, tokenizers, and filters provided by Lucene. It also covers how to create custom analyzers and mapping with different data types.

Chapter 3, Putting Elasticsearch into Action, introduces Elasticsearch Query-DSL, various queries, and the data sorting techniques. You will also learn how to perform CRUD operations with Elasticsearch using Elasticsearch Python and Java clients.

Chapter 4, Aggregations for Analytics, is all about the Elasticsearch aggregation framework for building analytics on data. It provides many fundamental as well complex examples of data analytics that can be built using a combination of full-text search, term-based search, and multi level aggregations. The user will master the aggregation module of Elasticsearch by learning a complete set of practical code examples that are covered using Python and Java clients.

Chapter 5, Data Looks Better on Maps: Master Geo-Spatiality, discusses geo-data concepts and covers the rich geo-search functionalities offered by Elasticsearch including how to create mappings for geo-points and geo-shapes data, indexing documents, geo-aggregations, and sorting data based on geo-distance. It includes code examples for the most widely used geo-queries in both Python and Java.

Chapter 6, Document Relationships in NoSQL World, focuses on the techniques offered by Elasticsearch to handle relational data using nested and parent-child relationships and creating a schema for the same using real-world examples. The reader will also learn how to create mappings based on relational data and write code for indexing and querying data using Python and Java APIs.

Chapter 7, Different Methods of Search and Bulk Operations, covers the different types of search and bulk APIs that every programmer needs to know while developing applications and working with large data sets. You will learn examples of bulk processing, multi-searches, and faster data reindexing using both Python and Java, which will help you throughout your journey with Elasticsearch.

Chapter 8, Controlling Relevancy, discusses the most important aspect of search engines — relevancy. It covers the powerful scoring capabilities available in Elasticsearch and practical examples that show how you can control the scoring process according to your needs.

Chapter 9, Cluster Scaling in Production Deployments, shows how to create Elasticsearch clusters and configure different types of nodes with the right resource allocations. It also focuses on cluster scalability using the best practices in production environment.

Chapter 10, Backups and Security, focuses on the different mechanisms of creating data backups of an Elasticsearch cluster and restoring them back into the same or an other cluster. A step-by-step guide to setting up NFS (Network File System) is also provided. Finally, you will learn about setting up Nginx to secure Elasticsearch and load balance requests.

What you need for this book

This book was written using Elasticsearch version 2.0.0, and all the examples and functions should work with it. Using Oracle Java 1.7 u55 and above is recommended for creating Elasticsearch clusters. In addition to this, you'll need a command that allows you to send HTTP requests, such as curl, which is available for most operating systems. In addition to this, this book covers all the examples using Python and Java.

For Java examples, you will need to have Java JDK (Java Development Kit) installed and an editor that will allow you to develop your code (such as Eclipse). Apache Maven has been used to build Java codes.

To run the Python examples, you will need Python 2.7 and above and will also need to install Elasticsearch-Py, the official Python client for Elasticsearch.

In addition to this, some chapters may require additional software such as Elasticsearch plugins and other software but it has been explicitly mentioned when certain types of software are needed.

Who this book is for

Anyone who wants to build efficient search and analytics applications can choose this book. It is also beneficial for skilled developers, especially ones experienced with Lucene or Solr, who now want to learn Elasticsearch quickly. A basic knowledge of Python or Java and Linux is expected.

In addition to this, readers who want to see how to improve their query relevancy, and how to use Elasticsearch Java and Python API, may find this book interesting and useful.

Conventions

In this book, you will find a number of text styles that distinguish between different kinds of information. Here are some examples of these styles and an explanation of their meaning.

Code words in text, database table names, folder names, filenames, file extensions, pathnames, dummy URLs, user input, and Twitter handles are shown as follows: "REST endpoints also enable users to make changes in clusters and indices settings dynamically rather than manually pushing configuration updates to all the nodes in a cluster by editing the `elasticsearch.yml` file and restarting the node."

A block of code is set as follows:

```
{
    "int_array": [1, 2,3],
    "string_array": ["Lucene" ,"Elasticsearch","NoSQL"],
    "boolean": true,
    "null": null,
    "number": 123,
    "object": {
      "a": "b",
      "c": "d",
      "e": "f"
    },
    "string": "Learning Elasticsearch"
}
```

Any command-line input or output is written as follows:

```
wget https://download.elastic.co/elasticsearch/elasticsearch/
elasticsearch-2.0.0.deb
sudo dpkg -i elasticsearch-2.0.0.deb
```

 Warnings or important notes appear in a box like this.

 Tips and tricks appear like this.

Reader feedback

Feedback from our readers is always welcome. Let us know what you think about this book—what you liked or disliked. Reader feedback is important for us as it helps us develop titles that you will really get the most out of.

To send us general feedback, simply e-mail feedback@packtpub.com, and mention the book's title in the subject of your message.

If there is a topic that you have expertise in and you are interested in either writing or contributing to a book, see our author guide at www.packtpub.com/authors.

Customer support

Now that you are the proud owner of a Packt book, we have a number of things to help you to get the most from your purchase.

Downloading the example code

You can download the example code files from your account at http://www.packtpub.com for all the Packt Publishing books you have purchased. If you purchased this book elsewhere, you can visit http://www.packtpub.com/support and register to have the files e-mailed directly to you.

Downloading the color images of this book

We also provide you with a PDF file that has color images of the screenshots/diagrams used in this book. The color images will help you better understand the changes in the output. You can download this file from http://www.packtpub.com/sites/default/files/downloads/B03461_ColorImages.pdf.

Errata

Although we have taken every care to ensure the accuracy of our content, mistakes do happen. If you find a mistake in one of our books—maybe a mistake in the text or the code—we would be grateful if you could report this to us. By doing so, you can save other readers from frustration and help us improve subsequent versions of this book. If you find any errata, please report them by visiting http://www.packtpub.com/submit-errata, selecting your book, clicking on the **Errata Submission Form** link, and entering the details of your errata. Once your errata are verified, your submission will be accepted and the errata will be uploaded to our website or added to any list of existing errata under the Errata section of that title.

To view the previously submitted errata, go to `https://www.packtpub.com/books/content/support` and enter the name of the book in the search field. The required information will appear under the **Errata** section.

Piracy

Piracy of copyrighted material on the Internet is an ongoing problem across all media. At Packt, we take the protection of our copyright and licenses very seriously. If you come across any illegal copies of our works in any form on the Internet, please provide us with the location address or website name immediately so that we can pursue a remedy.

Please contact us at `copyright@packtpub.com` with a link to the suspected pirated material.

We appreciate your help in protecting our authors and our ability to bring you valuable content.

Questions

If you have a problem with any aspect of this book, you can contact us at `questions@packtpub.com`, and we will do our best to address the problem.

1
Getting Started with Elasticsearch

Nowadays, search is one of the primary functionalities needed in every application; it can be fulfilled by Elasticsearch, which also has many other extra features. Elasticsearch, which is built on top of Apache Lucene, is an open source, distributable, and highly scalable search engine. It provides extremely fast searches and makes data discovery easy.

In this chapter, we will cover the following topics:

- Concepts and terminologies related to Elasticsearch
- Rest API and the JSON data structure
- Installing and configuring Elasticsearch
- Installing the Elasticsearch plugins
- Basic operations with Elasticsearch

Introducing Elasticsearch

Elasticsearch is a distributed, full text search and analytic engine that is build on top of Lucene, a search engine library written in Java, and is also a base for Solr. After its first release in 2010, Elasticsearch has been widely adopted by large as well as small organizations, including NASA, Wikipedia, and GitHub, for different use cases. The latest releases of Elasticsearch are focusing more on resiliency, which builds confidence in users being able to use Elasticsearch as a data storeage tool, apart from using it as a full text search engine. Elasticsearch ships with sensible default configurations and settings, and also hides all the complexities from beginners, which lets everyone become productive very quickly by just learning the basics.

The primary features of Elasticsearch

Lucene is a blazing fast search library but it is tough to use directly and has very limited features to scale beyond a single machine. Elasticsearch comes to the rescue to overcome all the limitations of Lucene. Apart from providing a simple HTTP/JSON API, which enables language interoperability in comparison to Lucene's bare Java API, it has the following main features:

- **Distributed**: Elasticsearch is distributed in nature from day one, and has been designed for scaling horizontally and not vertically. You can start with a single-node Elasticsearch cluster on your laptop and can scale that cluster to hundreds or thousands of nodes without worrying about the internal complexities that come with distributed computing, distributed document storage, and searches.

- **High Availability**: Data replication means having multiple copies of data in your cluster. This feature enables users to create highly available clusters by keeping more than one copy of data. You just need to issue a simple command, and it automatically creates redundant copies of the data to provide higher availabilities and avoid data loss in the case of machine failure.

- **REST-based**: Elasticsearch is based on REST architecture and provides API endpoints to not only perform CRUD operations over HTTP API calls, but also to enable users to perform cluster monitoring tasks using REST APIs. REST endpoints also enable users to make changes to clusters and indices settings dynamically, rather than manually pushing configuration updates to all the nodes in a cluster by editing the `elasticsearch.yml` file and restarting the node. This is possible because each resource (index, document, node, and so on) in Elasticsearch is accessible via a simple URI.

- **Powerful Query DSL**: Query DSL (domain-specific language) is a JSON interface provided by Elasticsearch to expose the power of Lucene to write and read queries in a very easy way. Thanks to the Query DSL, developers who are not aware of Lucene query syntaxes can also start writing complex queries in Elasticsearch.

- **Schemaless**: Being schemaless means that you do not have to create a schema with field names and data types before indexing the data in Elasticsearch. Though it is one of the most misunderstood concepts, this is one of the biggest advantages we have seen in many organizations, especially in e-commerce sectors where it's difficult to define the schema in advance in some cases. When you send your first document to Elasticsearch, it tries its best to parse every field in the document and creates a schema itself. Next time, if you send another document with a different data type for the same field, it will discard the document. So, Elasticsearch is not completely schemaless but its dynamic behavior of creating a schema is very useful.

There are many more features available in Elasticsearch, such as multitenancy and percolation, which will be discussed in detail in the next chapters.

Understanding REST and JSON

Elasticsearch is based on a REST design pattern and all the operations, for example, document insertion, deletion, updating, searching, and various monitoring and management tasks, can be performed using the REST endpoints provided by Elasticsearch.

What is REST?

In a REST-based web API, data and services are exposed as resources with URLs. All the requests are routed to a resource that is represented by a path. Each resource has a resource identifier, which is called as URI. All the potential actions on this resource can be done using simple request types provided by the HTTP protocol. The following are examples that describe how CRUD operations are done with REST API:

- To create the user, use the following:

  ```
  POST /user
  fname=Bharvi&lname=Dixit&age=28&id=123
  ```

- The following command is used for retrieval:

  ```
  GET /user/123
  ```

- Use the following to update the user information:

  ```
  PUT /user/123
  fname=Lavleen
  ```

- To delete the user, use this:

  ```
  DELETE /user/123
  ```

Many Elasticsearch users get confused between the POST and PUT request types. The difference is simple. POST is used to create a new resource, while PUT is used to update an existing resource. The PUT request is used during resource creation in some cases but it must have the complete URI available for this.

What is JSON?

All the real-world data comes in object form. Every entity (object) has some properties. These properties can be in the form of simple key value pairs or they can be in the form of complex data structures. One property can have properties nested into it, and so on.

Elasticsearch is a document-oriented data store where objects, which are called as documents, are stored and retrieved in the form of JSON. These objects are not only stored, but also the content of these documents gets indexed to make them searchable.

JavaScript Object Notation (JSON) is a lightweight data interchange format and, in the NoSQL world, it has become a standard data serialization format. The primary reason behind using it as a standard format is the language independency and complex nested data structure that it supports. JSON has the following data type support:

Array, Boolean, Null, Number, Object, and String

The following is an example of a JSON object, which is self-explanatory about how these data types are stored in key value pairs:

```
{
  "int_array": [1, 2,3],
  "string_array": ["Lucene" ,"Elasticsearch","NoSQL"],
  "boolean": true,
  "null": null,
  "number": 123,
  "object": {
    "a": "b",
    "c": "d",
    "e": "f"
  },
  "string": "Learning Elasticsearch"
}
```

Elasticsearch common terms

The following are the most common terms that are very important to know when starting with Elasticsearch:

- **Node**: A single instance of Elasticsearch running on a machine.
- **Cluster**: A cluster is the single name under which one or more nodes/ instances of Elasticsearch are connected to each other.
- **Document**: A document is a JSON object that contains the actual data in key value pairs.

- **Index**: A logical namespace under which Elasticsearch stores data, and may be built with more than one Lucene index using shards and replicas.

- **Doc types**: A doc type in Elasticsearch represents a class of similar documents. A type consists of a name, such as a user or a blog post, and a mapping, including data types and the Lucene configurations for each field. (An index can contain more than one type.)

- **Shard**: Shards are containers that can be stored on a single node or multiple nodes and are composed of Lucene segments. An index is divided into one or more shards to make the data distributable.

 A shard can be either primary or secondary. A primary shard is the one where all the operations that change the index are directed. A secondary shard is the one that contains duplicate data of the primary shard and helps in quickly searching the data as well as for high availability; in a case where the machine that holds the primary shard goes down, then the secondary shard becomes the primary automatically.

- **Replica**: A duplicate copy of the data living in a shard for high availability.

Understanding Elasticsearch structure with respect to relational databases

Elasticsearch is a search engine in the first place but, because of its rich functionality offerings, organizations have started using it as a NoSQL data store as well. However, it has not been made for maintaining the complex relationships that are offered by traditional relational databases.

If you want to understand Elasticsearch in relational database terms then, as shown in the following image, an index in Elasticsearch is similar to a database that consists of multiple types. A single row is represented as a document, and columns are similar to fields.

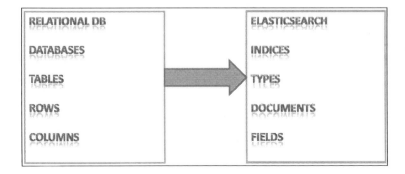

Elasticsearch does not have the concept of referential integrity constraints such as foreign keys. But, despite being a search engine and NoSQL data store, it does allow us to maintain some relationships among different documents, which will be discussed in the upcoming chapters.

With these theoretical concepts, we are good to go with learning the practical steps with Elasticsearch.

First of all, you need to be aware of the basic requirements to install and run Elasticsearch, which are listed as follows:

- Java (Oracle Java 1.7u55 and above)
- RAM: Minimum 2 GB
- Root permission to install and configure program libraries

 Please go through the following URL to check the JVM and OS dependencies of Elasticsearch: `https://www.elastic.co/subscriptions/matrix`.

The most common error that comes up if you are using an incompatible Java version with Elasticsearch, is the following:

```
Exception in thread "main" java.lang.UnsupportedClassVersionError: org/
elasticsearch/bootstrap/Elasticsearch : Unsupported major.minor version
51.0
    at java.lang.ClassLoader.defineClass1(Native Method)
    at java.lang.ClassLoader.defineClassCond(ClassLoader.java:637)
    at java.lang.ClassLoader.defineClass(ClassLoader.java:621)
    at java.security.SecureClassLoader.defineClass(SecureClassLoader.
java:141)
    at java.net.URLClassLoader.defineClass(URLClassLoader.java:283)
    at java.net.URLClassLoader.access$000(URLClassLoader.java:58)
    at java.net.URLClassLoader$1.run(URLClassLoader.java:197)
    at java.security.AccessController.doPrivileged(Native Method)
    at java.net.URLClassLoader.findClass(URLClassLoader.java:190)
    at java.lang.ClassLoader.loadClass(ClassLoader.java:306)
    at sun.misc.Launcher$AppClassLoader.loadClass(Launcher.java:301)
    at java.lang.ClassLoader.loadClass(ClassLoader.java:247)
```

If you see the preceding error while installing/working with Elasticsearch, it is most probably because you have an incompatible version of JAVA set as the JAVA_HOME variable or not set at all. Many users install the latest version of JAVA but forget to set the JAVA_HOME variable to the latest installation. If this variable is not set, then Elasticsearch looks into the following listed directories to find the JAVA and the first existing directory is used:

```
/usr/lib/jvm/jdk-7-oracle-x64, /usr/lib/jvm/java-7-oracle, /usr/lib/
jvm/java-7-openjdk, /usr/lib/jvm/java-7-openjdk-amd64/, /usr/lib/jvm/
java-7-openjdk-armhf, /usr/lib/jvm/java-7-openjdk-i386/, /usr/lib/jvm/
default-java
```

Installing and configuring Elasticsearch

I have used the Elasticsearch Version 2.0.0 in this book; you can choose to install other versions, if you wish to. You just need to replace the version number with 2.0.0. You need to have an administrative account to perform the installations and configurations.

Installing Elasticsearch on Ubuntu through Debian package

Let's get started with installing Elasticsearch on Ubuntu Linux. The steps will be the same for all Ubuntu versions:

1. Download the Elasticsearch Version 2.0.0 Debian package:

   ```
   wget https://download.elastic.co/elasticsearch/elasticsearch/
   elasticsearch-2.0.0.deb
   ```

2. Install Elasticsearch, as follows:

   ```
   sudo dpkg -i elasticsearch-2.0.0.deb
   ```

3. To run Elasticsearch as a service (to ensure Elasticsearch starts automatically when the system is booted), do the following:

   ```
   sudo update-rc.d elasticsearch defaults 95 10
   ```

Installing Elasticsearch on Centos through the RPM package

Follow these steps to install Elasticsearch on Centos machines. If you are using any other Red Hat Linux distribution, you can use the same commands, as follows:

1. Download the Elasticsearch Version 2.0.0 RPM package:

   ```
   wget https://download.elastic.co/elasticsearch/elasticsearch/
   elasticsearch-2.0.0.rpm
   ```

2. Install Elasticsearch, using this command:

   ```
   sudo rpm -i elasticsearch-2.0.0.rpm
   ```

3. To run Elasticsearch as a service (to ensure Elasticsearch starts automatically when the system is booted), use the following:

   ```
   sudo systemctl daemon-reload
   ```

   ```
   sudo systemctl enable elasticsearch.service
   ```

Understanding the Elasticsearch installation directory layout

The following table shows the directory layout of Elasticsearch that is created after installation. These directories, have some minor differences in paths depending upon the Linux distribution you are using.

Description	Path on Debian/Ubuntu	Path on RHEL/Centos
Elasticsearch home directory	/usr/share/elasticsearch	/usr/share/elasticsearch
Elasticsearch and Lucene jar files	/usr/share/elasticsearch/lib	/usr/share/elasticsearch/lib
Contains plugins	/usr/share/elasticsearch/plugins	/usr/share/elasticsearch/plugins
The locations of the binary scripts that are used to start an ES node and download plugins	usr/share/elasticsearch/bin	usr/share/elasticsearch/bin

Description	Path on Debian/Ubuntu	Path on RHEL/ Centos
Contains the Elasticsearch configuration files: (`elasticsearch.yml` and `logging.yml`)	`/etc/elasticsearch`	`/etc/ elasticsearch`
Contains the data files of the index/shard allocated on that node	`/var/lib/elasticsearch/data`	`/var/lib/ elasticsearch/ data`
The startup script for Elasticsearch (contains environment variables including HEAP SIZE and file descriptors)	`/etc/init.d/elasticsearch`	`/etc/sysconfig/ elasticsearch` Or `/etc/init.d/ elasticsearch`
Contains the log files of Elasticsearch.	`/var/log/elasticsearch/`	`/var/log/ elasticsearch/`

During installation, a user and a group with the `elasticsearch` name are created by default. Elasticsearch does not get started automatically just after installation. It is prevented from an automatic startup to avoid a connection to an already running node with the same cluster name.

It is recommended to change the cluster name before starting Elasticsearch for the first time.

Configuring basic parameters

1. Open the `elasticsearch.yml` file, which contains most of the Elasticsearch configuration options:

   ```
   sudo vim /etc/elasticsearch/elasticsearch.yml
   ```

2. Now, edit the following ones:

   - `cluster.name`: The name of your cluster
   - `node.name`: The name of the node
   - `path.data`: The path where the data for the ES will be stored

Similar to path.data, we can change path.logs and path.plugins as well. Make sure all these parameters values are inside double quotes.

3. After saving the elasticsearch.yml file, start Elasticsearch:

```
sudo service elasticsearch start
```

Elasticsearch will start on two ports, as follows:

- **9200**: This is used to create HTTP connections
- **9300**: This is used to create a TCP connection through a JAVA client and the node's interconnection inside a cluster

Do not forget to uncomment the lines you have edited. Please note that if you are using a new data path instead of the default one, then you first need to change the owner and the group of that data path to the user, *elasticsearch*.

The command to change the directory ownership to *elasticsearch* is as follows:

```
sudo chown -R elasticsearch:elasticsearch data_
directory_path
```

4. Run the following command to check whether Elasticsearch has been started properly:

```
sudo service elasticsearch status
```

If the output of the preceding command is shown as **elasticsearch is not running,** then there must be some configuration issue. You can open the log file and see what is causing the error.

The list of possible issues that might prevent Elasticsearch from starting is:

- A Java issue, as discussed previously
- Indention issues in the elasticsearch.yml file
- At least 1 GB of RAM is not free to be used by Elasticsearch
- The ownership of the data directory path is not changed to *elasticsearch*
- Something is already running on port 9200 or 9300

Adding another node to the cluster

Adding another node in a cluster is very simple. You just need to follow all the steps for installation on another system to install a new instance of Elasticsearch. However, keep the following in mind:

- In the `elasticsearch.yml` file, `cluster.name` is set to be the same on both the nodes
- Both the systems should be reachable from each other over the network.
- There is no firewall rule set for Elasticsearch port blocking
- The Elasticsearch and JAVA versions are the same on both the nodes

You can optionally set the `network.host` parameter to the IP address of the system to which you want Elasticsearch to be bound and the other nodes to communicate.

Installing Elasticsearch plugins

Plugins provide extra functionalities in a customized manner. They can be used to query, monitor, and manage tasks. Thanks to the wide Elasticsearch community, there are several easy-to-use plugins available. In this book, I will be discussing some of them.

The Elasticsearch plugins come in two flavors:

- **Site plugins**: These are the plugins that have a site (web app) in them and do not contain any Java-related content. After installation, they are moved to the site directory and can be accessed using `es_ip:port/_plugin/plugin_name`.
- **Java plugins**: These mainly contain `.jar` files and are used to extend the functionalities of Elasticsearch. For example, the Carrot2 plugin that is used for text-clustering purposes.

Elasticsearch ships with a plugin script that is located in the `/user/share/elasticsearch/bin` directory, and any plugin can be installed using this script in the following format:

```
bin/plugin --install plugin_url
```

> Once the plugin is installed, you need to restart that node to make it active. In the following image, you can see the different plugins installed inside the Elasticsearch node. Plugins need to be installed separately on each node of the cluster.

The following is the layout of the plugin directory of Elasticsearch:

```
bharvi@grownout:~$ cd /usr/share/elasticsearch/plugins/
bharvi@grownout:/usr/share/elasticsearch/plugins$ ls
carrot2  head  marvel
bharvi@grownout:/usr/share/elasticsearch/plugins$ cd carrot2/
bharvi@grownout:/usr/share/elasticsearch/plugins/carrot2$ ls
attributes-binder-1.2.2.jar      guava-18.0.jar              jackson-databind-2.5.3.jar  _site
carrot2-mini-3.10.1.jar          hppc-0.7.1.jar              mahout-collections-1.0.jar  slf4j-api-1.7.12.jar
commons-lang-2.6.jar             jackson-annotations-2.5.3.jar  mahout-math-0.6.jar       slf4j-log4j12-1.7.12.jar
elasticsearch-carrot2-1.9.0.jar  jackson-core-2.5.3.jar      simple-xml-2.7.jar
```

Checking for installed plugins

You can check the log of your node that shows the following line at start up time:

```
[2015-09-06 14:16:02,606][INFO ][plugins                    ] [Matt
Murdock] loaded [clustering-carrot2, marvel], sites [marvel, carrot2,
head]
```

Alternatively, you can use the following command:

```
curl XGET 'localhost:9200/_nodes/plugins'?pretty
```

Another option is to use the following URL in your browser:

```
http://localhost:9200/_nodes/plugins
```

Installing the Head plugin for Elasticsearch

The Head plugin is a web front for the Elasticsearch cluster that is very easy to use. This plugin offers various features such as showing the graphical representations of shards, the cluster state, easy query creations, and downloading query-based data in the CSV format.

The following is the command to install the Head plugin:

```
sudo /usr/share/elasticsearch/bin/plugin -install mobz/elasticsearch-head
```

Restart the Elasticsearch node with the following command to load the plugin:

```
sudo service elasticsearch restart
```

Once Elasticsearch is restarted, open the browser and type the following URL to access it through the Head plugin:

```
http://localhost:9200/_plugin/head
```

 More information about the Head plugin can be found here:
https://github.com/mobz/elasticsearch-head

Installing Sense for Elasticsearch

Sense is an awesome tool to query Elasticsearch. You can add it to your latest version of Chrome, Safari, or Firefox browsers as an extension.

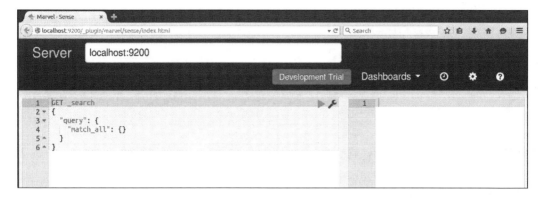

Now, when Elasticsearch is installed and running in your system, and you have also installed the plugins, you are good to go with creating your first index and performing some basic operations.

Basic operations with Elasticsearch

We have already seen how Elasticsearch stores data and provides REST APIs to perform the operations. In next few sections, we will be performing some basic actions using the command line tool called CURL. Once you have grasped the basics, you will start programming and implementing these concepts using Python and Java in upcoming chapters.

> When we create an index, Elasticsearch by default creates five shards and one replica for each shard (this means five primary and five replica shards). This setting can be controlled in the elasticsearch.yml file by changing the index.number_ of_shards properties and the index.number_of_replicas settings, or it can also be provided while creating the index.

Once the index is created, the number of shards can't be increased or decreased; however, you can increase or decrease the number of replicas at any time after index creation. So it is better to choose the number of required shards for an index at the time of index creation.

Creating an Index

Let's begin by creating our first index and give this index a name, which is book in this case. After executing the following command, an index with five shards and one replica will be created:

```
curl -XPUT 'localhost:9200/books/'
```

 Uppercase letters and blank spaces are not allowed in index names.

Indexing a document in Elasticsearch

Similar to all databases, Elasticsearch has the concept of having a unique identifier for each document that is known as _id. This identifier is created in two ways, either you can provide your own unique ID while indexing the data, or if you don't provide any id, Elasticsearch creates a default id for that document. The following are the examples:

```
curl -XPUT 'localhost:9200/books/elasticsearch/1' -d '{
"name":"Elasticsearch Essentials",
"author":"Bharvi Dixit",
"tags":["Data Analytics","Text Search","Elasticsearch"],
"content":"Added with PUT request"
}'
```

On executing above command, Elasticsearch will give the following response:

```
{"_index":"books","_type":"elasticsearch","_id":"1","_
version":1,"created":true}
```

However, if you do not provide an id, which is 1 in our case, then you will get the following error:

```
No handler found for uri [/books/elasticsearch] and method [PUT]
```

The reason behind the preceding error is that we are using a PUT request to create a document. However, Elasticsearch has no idea where to store this document (no existing URI for the document is available).

If you want the `_id` to be auto generated, you have to use a POST request. For example:

```
curl -XPOST 'localhost:9200/books/elasticsearch' -d '{
"name":"Elasticsearch Essentials",
"author":"Bharvi Dixit",
"tags":["Data Anlytics","Text Search","Elasticsearch"],
"content":"Added with POST request"
}'
```

The response from the preceding request will be as follows:

```
{"_index":"books","_type":"elasticsearch","_id":"AU-ityC8xdEEi6V7cMV5","_
version":1,"created":true}
```

If you open the `localhost:9200/_plugin/head` URL, you can perform all the CRUD operations using the HEAD plugin as well:

Some of the stats that you can see in the preceding image are these:

- Cluster name: `elasticsearch_cluster`
- Node name: `node-1`
- Index name: books
- No. of primary shards: 5
- No. of docs in the index: 2
- No. of unassigned shards (replica shards): 5

Cluster states in Elasticsearch

An Elasticsearch cluster can be in one of the three states: GREEN, YELLOW, or RED. If all the shards, meaning primary as well as replicas, are assigned in the cluster, it will be in the GREEN state. If any one of the replica shards is not assigned because of any problem, then the cluster will be in the YELLOW state. If any one of the primary shards is not assigned on a node, then the cluster will be in the RED state. We will see more on these states in the upcoming chapters. Elasticsearch never assigns a primary and its replica shard on the same node.

Fetching documents

We have stored documents in Elasticsearch. Now we can fetch them using their unique ids with a simple GET request.

Get a complete document

We have already indexed our document. Now, we can get the document using its document identifier by executing the following command:

```
curl -XGET 'localhost:9200/books/elasticsearch/1'?pretty
```

The output of the preceding command is as follows:

```
{
  "_index" : "books",
  "_type" : "elasticsearch",
  "_id" : "1",
  "_version" : 1,
  "found" : true,
  "_source":{"name":"Elasticsearch Essentials","author":"Bharvi Dixit",
"tags":["Data Anlytics","Text Search","ELasticsearch"],"content":"Added
with PUT request"}
}
```

pretty is used in the preceding request to make the response nicer and more readable.

As you can see, there is a _source field in the response. This is a special field reserved by Elasticsearch to store all the JSON data. There are options available to not store the data in this field since it comes with an extra disk space requirement. However, this also helps in many ways while returning data from ES, re-indexing data, or doing partial document updates. We will see more on this field in the next chapters.

If the document did not exist in the index, the _found field would have been marked as false.

Getting part of a document

Sometimes you need only some of the fields to be returned instead of returning the complete document. For these scenarios, you can send the names of the fields to be returned inside the _source parameter with the GET request:

```
curl -XGET 'localhost:9200/books/elasticsearch/1'?_source=name,author
```

The response of Elasticsearch will be as follows:

```
{
"_index":"books",
"_type":"elasticsearch",
"_id":"1",
"_version":1,
"found":true,
"_source":{"author":"Bharvi Dixit","name":"Elasticsearch Essentials"}
}
```

Updating documents

It is possible to update documents in Elasticsearch, which can be done either completely or partially, but updates come with some limitations and costs. In the next sections, we will see how these operations can be performed and how things work behind the scenes.

Updating a whole document

To update a whole document, you can use a similar PUT/POST request, which we had used to create a new document:

```
curl -XPUT 'localhost:9200/books/elasticsearch/1' -d '{
"name":"Elasticsearch Essentials",
"author":"Bharvi Dixit",
"tags":["Data Analytics","Text Search","Elasticsearch"],
"content":"Updated document",
"publisher":"pact-pub"
}'
```

The response of Elasticsearch looks like this:

```
{"_index":"books","_type":"elasticsearch","_id":"1","_
version":2,"created":false}
```

If you look at the response, it shows _version is 2 and created is false, meaning the document is updated.

Updating documents partially

Instead of updating the whole document, we can use the _update API to do partial updates. As shown in the following example, we will add a new field, updated_time, to the document for which a script parameter has been used. Elasticsearch uses Groovy scripting by default.

> Scripting is by default disabled in Elasticsearch, so to use a script you need to enable it by adding the following parameter to your elasticsearch.yml file:
>
> ```
> script.inline: on
> ```

```
curl -XPOST 'localhost:9200/books/elasticsearch/1/_update' -d '{

    "script" : "ctx._source.updated_time= \"2015-09-09T00:00:00\""

}'
```

The response of the preceding request will be this:

```
{"_index":"books","_type":"elasticsearch","_id":"1","_version":3}
```

It shows that a new version has been created in Elasticsearch.

Elasticsearch stores data in indexes that are composed of Lucene segments. These segments are immutable in nature, meaning that, once created, they can't be changed. So, when we send an update request to Elasticsearch, it does the following things in the background:

- Fetches the JSON data from the _source field for that document
- Makes changes in the _source field
- Deletes old documents
- Creates a new document

All these data re-indexing tasks can be done by the user; however, if you are using the UPDATE method, it is done using only one request. These processes are the same when doing a whole document update as for a partial update. The benefit of a partial update is that all operations are done within a single shard, which avoids network overhead.

Deleting documents

To delete a document using its identifier, we need to use the DELETE request:

```
curl -XDELETE 'localhost:9200/books/elasticsearch/1'
```

The following is the response of Elasticsearch:

```
{"found":true,"_index":"books","_type":"elasticsearch","_id":"1","_version":4}
```

If you are from a Lucene background, then you must know how segment merging is done and how new segments are created in the background with more documents getting indexed. Whenever we delete a document from Elasticsearch, it does not get deleted from the file system right away. Rather, Elasticsearch just marks that document as deleted, and when you index more data, segment merging is done. At the same time, the documents that are marked as deleted are indeed deleted based on a merge policy. This process is also applied while the document is updated.

The space from deleted documents can also be reclaimed with the _optimize API by executing the following command:

```
curl -XPOST http://localhost:9200/_optimize?only_expunge_deletes=true'
```

Checking documents' existence

While developing applications, some scenarios require you to check whether a document exists or not in Elasticsearch. In these scenarios, rather than querying the documents with a GET request, you have the option of using another HTTP request method called HEAD:

```
curl -i -XHEAD 'localhost:9200/books/elasticsearch/1'
```

The following is the response of the preceding command:

```
HTTP/1.1 200 OK

Content-Type: text/plain; charset=UTF-8

Content-Length: 0
```

In the preceding command, I have used the -i parameter that is used to show the header information of an HTTP response. It has been used because the HEAD request only returns headers and not any content. If the document is found, then status code will be 200, and if not, then it will be 400.

Summary

A lot of things have been covered in this chapter. You have got to know about the Elasticsearch architecture and its workings. Then, you have learned about the installations of Elasticsearch and its plugins. Finally, basic operations with Elasticsearch were done.

With all these, you are ready to learn about data analysis phases and mappings in the next chapter.

2
Understanding Document Analysis and Creating Mappings

Search is hard, and it becomes harder when both speed and relevancy are required together. There are lots of configurable options Elasticsearch provides out-of-the-box to take control before you start putting the data into it. *Elasticsearch is schemaless.* I gave a brief idea in the previous chapter of why it is not completely schemaless and how it creates a schema right after indexing the very first document for all the fields existing in that document. However, the schema matters a lot for a better and more relevant search. Equally important is understanding the theory behind the phases of document indexing and search.

In this chapter, we will cover the following topics:

- Full text search and inverted indices
- Document analysis
- Introducing Lucene analyzers
- Creating custom analyzers
- Elasticsearch mappings

Text search

Searching is broadly divided into two types: **exact term search** and **full text search**. An exact term search is something in which we look out for the exact terms; for example, any named entity such as the name of a person, location, or organization or date. These searches are easier to make since the search engine simply looks out for a yes or no and returns the documents.

However, full text search is different as well as challenging. Full text search refers to the search within text fields, where the text can be unstructured as well as structured. The text data can be in the form of any human language and based on the natural languages, which are very hard for a machine to understand and give relevant results. The following are some examples of full text searches:

- Find all the documents with *search* in the title or content fields, and return the results with matches in titles with the higher score

- Find all the tweets in which people are talking about *terrorism* and *killing* and return the results sorted by the tweet creation time

While doing these kinds of searches, we not only want relevant results but also expect that the search for a keyword matches all of its synonyms, root words, and spelling mistakes. For example, terrorism should match terorism and terror, while killing should match kills, kill, and killed.

To serve all these queries, the text-based fields go through an analysis phase before indexing, and based on this analysis, inverted indexes are built. At the time of querying, the same analysis process is applied to the terms that are sent within the queries to match those terms stored in the inverted indexes.

TF-IDF

TF-IDF stands for **term frequencies-inverse document frequencies**, and it is an important parameter used inside Lucene's standard similarity algorithm, **Vector Space Model (VSM)**. The weight calculated by TF-IDF is the statistical measure to evaluate how important a word is to a document in a collection of documents.

Let's see how a TF-IDF weight is calculated to find our term's relevancy:

- **TF (term)**: (The number of times a term appears in a document) / (The total number of terms in the document)

- **IDF (term)**: $\log_e$ (The total number of documents / The number of documents with the t term in it)

While calculating IDF, the log is taken because terms such as *the*, *that*, and *is* may appear too many times, and we need to weigh down these frequently appearing terms while increasing the importance of rare terms.

The weight of TF-IDF is a product of *TF(term)*IDF(term)*.

In information retrieval, one of the simplest relevancy ranking functions is implemented by summing the TF-IDF weight for each query term. Based on the combined weights for all the terms appearing in a single query, a score is calculated that is used to return the results in a sorted order.

Inverted indexes

Inverted index is the heart of search engines. The primary goal of a search engine is to provide speedy searches while finding the documents in which our search terms occur. Relevancy comes second.

Let's see with an example how inverted indexes are created and why they are so fast. In this example, we have two documents with each content field containing the following texts:

- I hate when spiders sit on the wall and act like they pay rent
- I hate when spider just sit there

While indexing, these texts are tokenized into separate terms and all the unique terms are stored inside the index with information such as in which document this term appears and what is the term position in that document.

The inverted index built with the preceding document texts looks like this:

Term	Document:Position
I	1:1, 2:1
Hate	1:2, 2:2
When	1:3, 2:3
Spiders	1:4
Sit	1:5, 2:5
On	1:6
Wall	1:7
Spider	2:4

Term	Document:Position
Just	2:5
There	2:6

When you search for the term spider OR spiders, the query is executed against the inverted index and the terms are looked out for, and the documents where these terms appear are quickly identified. If you search for spider AND spiders, you will not get any results because when we use AND queries, both the terms used in the queries must be present in the document. However, spiders and spider are different for the search engine unless they are normalized into their root forms. For all these term normalizations, Elasticsearch has a document analysis phase that we will see in the upcoming sections.

Document analysis

When we index documents into Elasticsearch, it goes through an analysis phase that is necessary in order to create inverted indexes. It is a series of steps performed by Lucene, which is depicted in the following image:

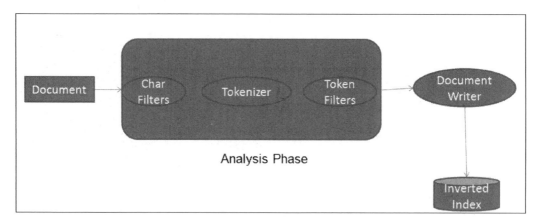

The analysis phase is performed by analyzers that are composed of one or more char filters, a single tokenizer, and one or more token filters. You can declare separate analyzers for each field in your document depending on the need. For the same field, the analyzers can be the same for both indexing and searching or they can be different.

- **Character Filters**: The job of character filters is to do cleanup tasks such as stripping out HTML tags.

- **Tokenizers**: The next step is to split the text into terms that are called tokens. This is done by a tokenizer. The splitting can be done based on any rule such as whitespace. More details about tokenizers can be found at this URL: `https://www.elastic.co/guide/en/elasticsearch/reference/current/analysis-tokenizers.html`.

- **Token filters**: Once the tokens are created, they are passed to token filters that normalize the tokens. Token filters can change the tokens, remove the terms, or add terms to new tokens.

The most used token filters are: the lowercase token filter, which converts a token into lowercase: the stop token filter, which removes the stop word tokens such as to, be, a, an, the, and so on: and the ASCII folding token filter, which converts Unicode characters into their ASCII equivalent. A long list of token filters can be found here: `https://www.elastic.co/guide/en/elasticsearch/reference/current/analysis-tokenfilters.html`.

Introducing Lucene analyzers

Lucene has a wide range of built-in analyzers. We will see the most important ones here:

- **Standard analyzer**: This is the default analyzer used by Elasticsearch unless you mention any other analyzer to be used explicitly. This is best suited for any language. A standard analyzer is composed of a standard tokenizer (which splits the text as defined by Unicode Standard Annex), a standard token filter, a lowercase token filter, and a stop token filter.

> A standard tokenizer uses a stop token filter but it defaults to an empty stopword list, so it does not remove any stop words by default. If you need to remove stopwords, you can either use the stop analyzer or you can provide a stopword list to the standard analyzer setting.

- **Simple analyzer**: A simple analyzer splits the token wherever it finds a non-letter character and lowercases all the terms using the lowercase token filter.

- **Whitespace analyzer**: As the name suggests, it splits the text at white spaces. However, unlike simple and standard analyzers, it does not lowercase tokens.

- **Keyword analyzer**: A keyword analyzer creates a single token of the entire stream. Similar to the whitespace analyzer, it also does not lowercase tokens. This analyzer is good for fields such as zip codes and phone numbers. It is mainly used for either exact terms matching, or while doing aggregations. However, it is beneficial to use `not_analyzed` for these kinds of fields.

- **Language analyzer**: There are lots of ready-made analyzers available for many languages. These analyzers understand the grammatical rules and the stop words of corresponding languages, and create tokens accordingly. To know more about language specific analyzers, visit the following URL: `https://www.elastic.co/guide/en/elasticsearch/reference/current/analysis-lang-analyzer.html`.

Elasticsearch provides an easy way to test the analyzers with the `_analyze` REST endpoint. Just create a test index, as follows:

```
curl -XPUT 'localhost:9200/test'
```

Use the following command by passing the text through the `_analyze` API to test the analyzer regarding how your tokens will be created:

```
curl -XGET 'localhost:9200/test/_analyze?analyzer=whitespace&text=testi
ng, Analyzers&pretty'
```

You will get the following response:

```
{
  "tokens" : [ {
    "token" : "testing,",
    "start_offset" : 0,
    "end_offset" : 8,
    "type" : "word",
    "position" : 1
  }, {
    "token" : "Analyzers",
    "start_offset" : 9,
    "end_offset" : 18,
    "type" : "word",
    "position" : 2
  } ]
}
```

You can see in the response how Elasticsearch splits the `testing` and `Analyzers` text into two tokens based on white spaces. It also returns the token positions and the offsets. You can hit the preceding request in your favorite browser too using this: `localhost:9200/test/_analyze?analyzer=whitespace&text=testing, Analyzers&pretty`.

The following image explains how different analyzers split a token and how many tokens they produce for the same stream of text:

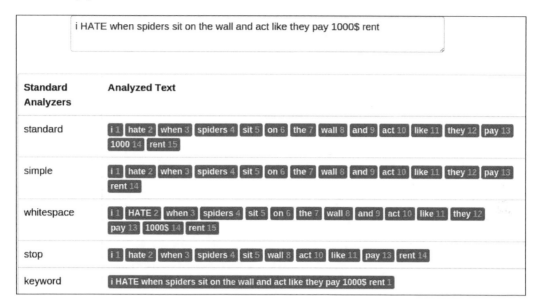

Creating custom analyzers

In the previous section, we saw in-built analyzers. Sometimes, they are not good enough to serve our purpose. We need to customize the analyzers using built-in tokenizers and token/char filters. For example, the keyword analyzer by default does not use a lowercase filter, but we need it so that data is indexed in the lowercase form and is searched using either lowercase or uppercase.

To achieve this purpose, Elasticsearch provides a custom analyzer that's type is custom and can be combined with one tokenizer with zero or more token filters and zero or more char filters.

Custom analyzers always take the following form:

```
{
  "analysis": {
    "analyzer": {}, //Where we put our custom analyzers
    "filters": {} //where we put our custom filters.
  }
}
```

Let's create a custom analyzer now with the name `keyword_tokenizer` using the keyword tokenizer and lowercase and asciifolding token filters:

```
"keyword_tokenizer": {
  "type": "custom",
    "filter": [
      "lowercase",
      "asciifolding"
    ],
    "tokenizer": "keyword"
}
```

Similarly, we can create one more custom analyzer with the name `url_analyzer` for creating tokens of URLs and e-mail addresses:

```
"url_analyzer": {
        "type": "custom",
        "filter": [
          "lowercase",
          "stop"
        ],
        "tokenizer": "uax_url_email"
}
```

Changing a default analyzer

You have all the control to define the type of analyzer to be used for each field while creating mapping. However, what about those dynamic fields that you do not know about while creating mappings. By default, these fields will be indexed with a standard analyzer. But in case you want to change this default behavior, you can do it in the following way.

A default analyzer always has the name default and is created using a custom type:

```
"default": {
      "filter": [
        "standard",
        "lowercase",
        "asciifolding"
      ],
      "type": "custom",
      "tokenizer": "keyword"
}
```

In the preceding setting, the name of the `analyzer` is default, which is created with the keyword tokenizer.

Putting custom analyzers into action

We have learned to create custom analyzers but we have to tell Elasticsearch about our custom analyzers so that they can be used. This can be done via the `_settings` API of Elasticsearch, as shown in the following example:

```
curl -XPUT 'localhost/index_name/_settings' -d '{
  "analysis": {
    "analyzer": {
      "default": {
        "filter": [
          "standard",
          "lowercase",
          "asciifolding"
        ],
        "type": "custom",
        "tokenizer": "keyword"
      }
    },
    "keyword_tokenizer": {
      "filter": [
        "lowercase",
        "asciifolding"
      ],
      "type": "custom",
      "tokenizer": "keyword"
    }
  }
}'
```

> If an index already exists and needs to be updated with new custom analyzers, then the index first needs to be closed before updating the analyzers. It can be done using `curl -XPOST 'localhost:9200/index_name/_close'`. After updating, the index can be opened again using `curl -XPOST 'localhost:9200/index_name/_open'`.

Elasticsearch mapping

We have seen in the previous chapter how an index can have one or more types and each type has its own mapping.

Mappings are like database schemas that describe the fields or properties that the documents of that type may have. For example, the data type of each field, such as a string, integer, or date, and how these fields should be indexed and stored by Lucene.

One more thing to consider is that unlike a database, you cannot have a field with the same name with different types in the same index; otherwise, you will break doc_values, and the sorting/searching is also broken. For example, create myIndex and also index a document with a valid field that contains an integer value inside the type1 document type:

```
curl -XPOST localhost:9200/myIndex/type1/1 -d '{"valid":5}'
```

Now, index another document inside type2 in the same index with the valid field. This time the valid field contains a string value:

```
curl -XPOST localhost/myIndex/type2/1 -d '{"valid":"40"}'
```

In this scenario, the sort and aggregations on the valid field are broken because they are both indexed as valid fields in the same index!

Document metadata fields

When a document is indexed into Elasticsearch, there are several metadata fields maintained by Elasticsearch for that document. The following are the most important metadata fields you need to know in order to control your index structure:

- _id: _id is a unique identifier for the document and can be either auto-generated or can be set while indexing or can be configured in the mapping to be parsed automatically from a field.

- _source: This is a special field generated by Elasticsearch that contains the actual JSON data in it. Whenever we execute a search request, the _source field is returned by default. By default, it is enabled, but it can be disabled using the following configuration while creating a mapping:

```
PUT index_name/_mapping/doc_type
        {"_source":{"enabled":false}}
```

 Be careful while disabling the _source field, as there are lots of features you can't with it disabled. For example, highlighting is dependent on the _source field. Documents can only be searched and not returned; documents can't be re-indexed and can't be updated.

- _all: When a document is indexed, values from all the fields are indexed separately as well as in a special field called _all. This is done by Elasticsearch by default to make a search request on the content of the document without specifying the field name. It comes with an extra storage cost and should be disabled if searches need to be made against field names. For disabling it completely, use the following configuration in you mapping file:

```
PUT index_name/_mapping/doc_type
    {"_all": { "enabled": true  }}
```

However, there are some cases where you do not want to include all the fields to be included in _all where only certain fields. You can achieve it by setting the include_in_all parameter to false:

```
PUT index_name/_mapping/doc_type
    {
        "_all": {
        "enabled": true
        },
        "properties": {
          "first_name": {
          "type": "string",
          "include_in_all": false
          },
          "last_name": {
          "type": "string"
          }
        }
    }
```

In the preceding example, only the last name will be included inside the _all field.

- _ttl: There are some cases when you want the documents to be automatically deleted from the index. For example, the logs. _ttl (time to live) field provides the options you can set when the documents should be deleted automatically. By default, it is disabled and can be enabled using the following configuration:

```
PUT index_name/_mapping/doc_type
{
  "_ttl": {
    "enabled": true,
    "default": "1w"
    }
}
```

Inside the default field, you can use time units such as m (minutes), d (days), w (weeks), M (months), and ms (milliseconds). The default is milliseconds.

 Please note that the __ttl field has been deprecated since the Elasticsearch 2.0.0 beta 2 release and might be removed from the upcoming versions. Elasticsearch will provide a new replacement for this field in future versions.

- dynamic: There are some scenarios in which you want to restrict the dynamic fields to be indexed. You only allow the fields that are defined by you in the mapping. This can be done by setting the dynamic property to be strict, in the following way:

```
PUT index_name/_mapping/doc_type
{
    "dynamic": "strict",
    "properties": {
      "first_name": {
      "type": "string"
      },
      "last_name": {
      "type": "string"
      }
    }
}
```

Data types and index analysis options

Lucene provides several options to configure each and every field separately depending on the use case. These options slightly differ based on the data types for a field.

Configuring data types

Data types in Elasticsearch are segregated in two forms:

- **Core types**: These include string, number, date, boolean, and binary
- **Complex data types**: These include arrays, objects, multi fields, geo points, geo shapes, nested, attachment, and IP

 Since Elasticsearch understands JSON, all the data types supported by JSON are also supported in Elasticsearch, along with some extra data types such as geopoint and attachment.

The following are the common attributes for the core data types:

- `index`: The values can be from `analyzed`, `no`, or `not_analyzed`. If set to `analyzed`, the text for that field is analyzed using a specified analyzer. If set to `no`, the values for that field do not get indexed and thus, are not searchable. If set to `not_analyzed`, the values are indexed as it is; for example, `Elasticsearch Essentials` will be indexed as a single term and thus, only exact matches can be done while querying.

- `store`: This takes values as either yes or no (default is `no` but `_source` is an exception). Apart from indexing the values, Lucene does have an option to store the data, which comes in handy when you want to extract the data from the field. However, since Elasticsearch has an option to store all the data inside the `_source` field, it is usually not required to store individual fields in Lucene.

- `boost`: This defaults to `1`. This specifies the importance of the field inside doc.

- `null_value`: Using this attribute, you can set a default value to be indexed if a document contains a null value for that field. The default behavior is to omit the field that contains null.

> One should be careful while configuring default values for null. The default value should always be of the type corresponding to the data type configured for that field, and it also should not be a real value that might appear in some other document.

Let's start with the configuration of the core as well as complex data types.

String

In addition to the common attributes, the following attributes can also be set for string-based fields:

- `term_vector`: This property defines whether the Lucene term vectors should be calculated for that field or not. The values can be `no` (the default one), `yes`, `with_offsets`, `with_positions`, and `with_positions_offsets`.

> A term vector is the list of terms in the document and their number of occurrences in that document. Term vectors are mainly used for Highlighting and MorelikeThis (searching for similar documents) queries. A very nice blog on term vectors has been written by Adrien Grand, which can be read here: `http://blog.jpountz.net/post/41301889664/putting-term-vectors-on-a-diet`.

- `omit_norms`: This takes values as `true` or `false`. The default value is `false`. When this attribute is set to `true`, it disables the Lucene norms calculation for that field (and thus you can't use index-time boosting).

- `analyzer`: A globally defined analyzer name for the index is used for indexing and searching. It defaults to the standard analyzer, but can be controlled also, which we will see in the upcoming section.

- `index_analyzer`: The name of the analyzer used for indexing. This is not required if the analyzer attribute is set.

- `search_analyzer`: The name of the analyzer used for searching. This is not required if the analyzer attribute is set.

- `ignore_above`: This specifies the maximum size of the field. If the character count is above the specified limit, that field won't be indexed. This setting is mainly used for the `not_analyzed` fields. Lucene has a term byte-length limit of 32,766. This means a single term cannot contain more than 10,922 characters (one UTF-8 character contains at most 3 bytes).

An example mapping for two string fields, `content` and `author_name`, is as follows:

```
{
  "contents": {
    "type": "string",
    "store": "yes",
    "index": "analyzed",
    "include_in_all": false,
    "analyzer": "simple"
  },
  "author_name": {
    "type": "string",
    "index": "not_analyzed",
    "ignore_above": 50
  }
}
```

Number

The number data types are: `byte`, `short`, `integer`, `long`, `floats`, and `double`. The fields that contain numeric values need to be configured with the appropriate data type. Please go through the storage type requirements for all the types under a number before deciding which type you should actually use. In case the field does not contain bigger values, choosing long instead of integer is a waste of space.

An example of configuring numeric fields is shown here:

```
{"price":{"type":"float"},"age":{"type":"integer"}}
```

Date

Working with dates usually comes with some extra challenges because there are so many data formats available and you need to decide the correct format while creating a mapping. Date fields usually take two parameters: type and format. However, you can use other analysis options too.

Elasticsearch provides a list of formats to choose from depending on the date format of your data. You can visit the following URL to learn more about it: http://www.elasticsearch.org/guide/reference/mapping/date-format.html.

The following is an example of configuring date fields:

```
{
  "creation_time": {
    "type": "date",
    "format": "YYYY-MM-dd"
  },
  "updation_time": {
    "type": "date",
    "format": "yyyy/MM/dd HH:mm:ss||yyyy/MM/dd"
  },
  "indexing_time": {
    "type": "date",
    "format": "date_optional_time"
  }
}
```

Please note the different date formats used for different date fields in the preceding mapping. The updation_time field contains a special format with an || operator, which specifies that it will work for both yyyy/MM/dd HH:mm:ss and yyyy/MM/dd date formats. Elasticsearch uses date_optional_time as the default date parsing format, which is an ISO datetime parser.

Boolean

While indexing data, a Boolean type field can contain only two values: true or false, and it can be configured in a mapping in the following way:

```
{"is_verified":{"type":"boolean"}}
```

Arrays

By default, all the fields in Lucene and thus in Elasticsearch are multivalued, which means that they can store multiple values. In order to send such fields for indexing to Elasticsearch, we use the JSON array type, which is nested within opening and closing square brackets []. Some considerations need to be taken care of while working with array data types:

- All the values of an array must be of the same data type.

- If the data type of a field is not explicitly defined in a mapping, then the data type of the first value inside the array is used as the type of that field.

- The order of the elements is not maintained inside the index, so do not get upset if you do not find the desired results while querying. However, this order is maintained inside the _source field, so when you return the data after querying, you get the same JSON as you had indexed.

Objects

JSON documents are hierarchical in nature, which allows them to define inner *objects*. Elasticsearch completely understands the nature of these inner objects and can map them easily by providing query support for their inner fields.

 Once a field is declared as an object type, you can't put any other type of data into it. If you try to do so, Elasticsearch will throw an exception.

```
{
  "features": {
    "type": "object",
    "properties": {
      "name": {
        "type": "string"
      },
      "sub_features": {
        "dynamic": false,
        "type": "object",
        "properties": {
          "name": {
            "type": "string"
          },
          "description": {
            "type": "string"
```

```
              }
            }
          }
        }
      }
    }
```

If you look carefully in the previous mapping, there is a `features` root object field and it contains two properties: `name` and `sub_features`. Further, `sub_features`, which is an inner object, also contains two properties: `name` and `description`, but it has an extra setting: `dynamic: false`. Setting this property to `false` for an object changes the dynamic behavior of Elasticsearch, and you cannot index any other fields inside that object apart from the one that is declared inside the mapping. Therefore, you can index more fields in future inside the features object, but not inside the `sub_features` object.

Indexing the same field in different ways

If you need to index the same field in different ways, the following is the way to create a mapping for it. You can define as many fields with the `fields` parameter as you want:

```
{
  "name": {
    "type": "string",
    "fields": {
      "raw": {
        "type": "string",
        "index": "not_analyzed"
      }
    }
  }
}
```

With the preceding mapping, you just need to index data into the `name` field, and Elasticsearch will index the data into the `name` field using the standard analyzer that can be used for a full text search, and the data in the `name.raw` field without analyzing the tokens; which can be used for an exact term matching. You do not have to send data into the `name.raw` field explicitly.

 Please note that this option is only available for core data types and not for the objects.

Putting mappings in an index

There are two ways of putting mappings inside an index:

- Using a post request at the time of index creation:

```
curl -XPOST 'localhost:9200/index_name' -d '{
  "settings": {
    "number_of_shards": 1,
    "number_of_replicas": 0
  },
  "mappings": {
    "type1": {
      "_all": {
        "enabled": false
      },
      "properties": {
        "field1": {
          "type": "string",
          "index": "not_analyzed"
        }
      }
    },
    "type2": {
      "properties": {
        "field2": {
          "type": "string",
          "index": "analyzed",
          "analyzer":"keyword"
        }
      }
    }
  }
}'
```

- Using a PUT request using the _mapping API. The index must exist before creating a mapping in this way:

```
curl -XPUT 'localhost:9200/index_name/index_type/_mapping' -d '{
"_all": {
        "enabled": false
    },
  "properties": {
    "field1": {
      "type": "integer"
    }
  }
}'
```

The mappings for the fields are enclosed inside the `properties` object, while all the metadata fields will appear outside the properties object.

 It is highly recommended to use the same configuration for the same field names across different types and indexes in a cluster. For instance, the data types and analysis options must be the same; otherwise, you will face weird outputs.

Viewing mappings

Mappings can be viewed easily with the `_mapping` API:

- To view the mapping of all the types in an index, use the following URL:
  `curl -XGET localhost:9200/index_name/_mapping?pretty`
- To view the mapping of a single type, use the following URL: `curl -XGET localhost:9200/index_name/type_name/_mapping?pretty`

Updating mappings

If you want to add mapping for some new fields in the mapping of an existing type, or create a mapping for a new type, you can do it later using the same `_mapping` API.

For example, to add a new field in our existing type, we only need to specify the mapping for the new field in the following way:

```
curl -XPUT 'localhost:9200/index_name/index_type/_mapping' -d '{
  "properties": {
    "new_field_name": {
      "type": "integer"
    }
  }
}'
```

Please note that the mapping definition of an existing field cannot be changed.

Dealing with a long JSON data to be sent in request body

While creating indexes with settings, custom analyzers, and mappings, you must have noted that all the JSON configurations are passed using −d, which stands for data. This is used to send a request body. While creating settings and mappings, it usually happens that the JSON data becomes so large that it gets difficult to use them in a command line using curl. The easy solution is to create a file with the .json extension and provide the path of the file while working with those settings or mappings. The following is an example command:

```
curl -XPUT 'localhost:9200/index_name/_settings' -d @
path/setting.json

curl -XPUT 'localhost:9200/index_name/index_type/_
mapping' -d @path/mapping.json
```

Summary

In this chapter, we covered a lot of ground involving inverted indexes, document analysis phases, the working of analyzers, and creating custom analyzers. We also learned about creating and working with mappings of different data types.

In the next chapter, we will start pushing data into Elasticsearch and will learn how to perform operations with Elasticsearch using Python and Java API.

3
Putting Elasticsearch into Action

We have covered a lot of ground on Elasticsearch architecture, indexes, analyzers, and mappings. It's time to start learning about the indexing of data and the querying of Elasticsearch using its rich *Query-DSL*.

In this chapter, we will cover the following topics:

- CRUD operations using the Elasticsearch Python client
- CRUD operations using the Elasticsearch Java client
- Creating a search database
- Introducing Query-DSL
- Search requests using Python
- Search requests using Java
- Sorting data
- Document routing

CRUD operations using elasticsearch-py

Elasticsearch is written in Java but it is interoperable with non-JVM languages too. In this book, we will use its Python client, `elasticsearch-py`, as well as its Java client to perform all the operations. The best part of this Python client library is that it communicates over HTTP and gives you the freedom to write your settings, mappings, and queries using plain JSON objects, and allows them to pass into the body parameters of the requests. To read more about this client, you can visit this URL: `http://elasticsearch-py.readthedocs.org/en/master/`.

All the examples used in this book are based on Python 2.7. However, they are compatible with Python version 3 also.

Setting up the environment

In this section, you will learn how to set up Python environments on Ubuntu using `pip` and `virtualenv`.

Installing Pip

`Pip` is a package installer for Python modules. It can be installed using the following commands:

```
sudo apt-get install python-pip python-dev build-essential
sudo pip install --upgrade pip
```

Installing virtualenv

While developing programs using Python, it is good practice to create `virtualenv`. A `virtualenv` command creates a directory that stores a private copy of Python and all the default Python packages. Virtual environments are of great help while working with several projects and different versions of Python on a single system. You can create separate virtual environments for each project and enable them for each corresponding project. To install `virtualenv`, use the following command:

```
sudo pip install --upgrade virtualenv
```

Once the virtual environment is installed, you can create a directory and copy existing Python packages to it using this command:

```
mkdir venv
virtualenv venv
```

After this, you can activate this environment with the following command:

```
source venv
```

Once this environment is activated, all the packages that you install will be inside this `venv` directory. A virtual environment can be deactivated using just the `deactivate` command.

Installing elasticsearch-py

`elasticsearch-py` can be easily installed using `pip` in the following way:

`pip install elasticsearch`

You can verify the installation using the following command:

`pip freeze | grep elasticsearch`

You will get to know which version of the Elasticsearch client has been installed:

`elasticsearch==1.6.0`

> The version can be different depending on the latest release. The preceding command installs the latest version. If you want to install a specific version, then you can specify the version using the `==` operator. For example, `pip install elasticsearch==1.5`.

Performing CRUD operations

You will learn to perform CRUD operations in the upcoming sections, but before that, let's start with the creation of indexes using Python code.

> Since `elasticsearch-py` communicates over HTTP, it takes JSON data (setting, mapping, and queries) in the body parameters of the requests. It is advisable to use a `sense` plugin (which comes with `Marvel` or as an extension too) to write queries, settings, mappings, and all other requests, because `sense` offers a lot of help with its autosuggestion functionality. Once the correct JSON data is created, you can simply store it inside a variable in your Python code and use it inside a function's body parameter.

Request timeouts

The default timeout for any request sent to Elasticsearch is 10 seconds but there are chances for requests not to get completed within 10 seconds due to the complexity of the queries, the load on Elasticsearch, or network latencies. You have two options to control the timeouts:

- **Global timeout**: This involves using the `timeout` parameter while creating a connection.
- **Per-request timeout**: This involves using the `request_timeout` parameter (in seconds) while hitting separate requests. When `request_timeout` is used, it overrides the global `timeout` value for that particular request.

Creating indexes with settings and mappings

Create a Python file with index settings and mappings and save it with the name config.py. It will have two variables, index_settings and doc_mappings:

```python
index_settings = {
"number_of_shards": 1,
"number_of_replicas": 1,
"index": {
"analysis": {
"analyzer": {
"keyword_analyzed": {
"type": "custom",
"filter": [
"lowercase",
"asciifolding"
],
"tokenizer": "keyword"
}
                }
            }
        }
    }
}
doc_mapping = {
"_all": {
"enabled": False
},
"properties": {
"skills": {
"type": "string",
"index": "analyzed",
"analyzer": "standard",
        }
    }
}
```

Now create another file, es_operations.py, and follow these steps:

1. Import the Elasticsearch module to your Python file:

   ```python
   from elasticsearch import Elasticsearch
   from time import time
   ```

2. Import the index_setting and mapping variables from the config file:

   ```python
   from config import index_settings, doc_mapping
   ```

3. Initialize the client:

```
es = Elasticsearch('localhost:9200')
```

4. Declare variables for the index name, doc type, and body. The body will contain the settings and the mapping:

```
index_name='books'
doc_type='search'
body = {}
mapping = {}
mapping[doc_type] = doc_mapping
body['settings'] = index_settings
body['mappings'] = mapping
```

5. Check whether the index exists; otherwise, create the index:

```
if not es.indices.exists(index = index_name):
print 'index does not exist, creating the index'
es.indices.create(index = index_name, body = body)
    time.sleep(2)
print 'index created successfully'
else:
print 'An index with this name already exists'
```

Indexing documents

Let's create a document and store it inside a `doc1` variable, which is a dictionary:

```
doc1 = {
'name' : 'Elasticsearch Essentials',
'category' : ['Big Data', 'search engines', 'Analytics'],
'Publication' : 'Packt-Pub',
'Publishing Date' : '2015-31-12'
}
```

Once the document is created, it can be indexed using the `index` function:

```
es.index(index = index_name, doc_type = doc_type, body = doc1, id = '123')
```

 If you want the unique ID to be autogenerated, use the None keyword inside the `id` parameter.

Retrieving documents

Document retrieval is done using a GET request that takes the following parameter:

```
response = es.get(index=index_name, doc_type=doc_type, id='1',
ignore=404)
print response
```

The `ignore` parameter is used to avoid exceptions in case the document does not exist in the index. The response will look as follows:

{u'_type': u'1', u'_source': {u'category': [u'Big Data', u'search engines', u'Analytics'], u'name': u'Elasticsearch Essentials', u'Publishing D
ate': u'2015-31-12', u'Publication': u'Packt-Pub'}, u'_index': u'1', u'_version': 1, u'found': True, u'_id': u'1'}
[u'Big Data', u'search engines', u'Analytics']

> In the response, all the field names start with u that denotes Unicode. In normal scenarios, this format does not affect when any task is performed with the response data. However, in some cases, you might require this to be in the form of a plain JSON format. To do this, simply import the JSON module of Python in your code and call the `json.dumps(response)` function with the response object inside its parameter.

All the fields are returned inside the `_source` object and a particular field can be accessed using this:

```
response.get('_source').get(field_name)
```

Updating documents

As we have seen in *Chapter 1, Getting Started with Elasticsearch*, a partial document update can be done using scripts with the `_update` API. With a Python client, it can be done using the `update` function. We can do an update in two scenarios; either to completely replace the value for a field, or to append the value inside that field. To use scripts to update the documents, make sure you have dynamic scripting enabled.

Replacing the value of a field completely

To replace the value of an existing field, you need to simply pass the new value inside the `_source` of the document in the following way:

```
script ={"script" : "ctx._source.category= \"data analytics\""}
es.update(index=index_name, doc_type=doc_type, body=script, id='1',
ignore=404)
```

After this request, the `category` field will contain only one value, `data analytics`.

Appending a value in an array

Sometimes you need to preserve the original value and append some new data inside it. Groovy scripting supports the use of parameters with the `param` attribute inside scripts, which helps us to achieve this task:

```
script =  {"script" : "ctx._source.category += tag",
"params" : {
"tag" : "Python"
}
        }
es.update(index=index_name, doc_type=doc_type, body=script, id='1',
ignore=404)
```

After this request, the `category` field will contain two values: `data analytics` and `Python`.

Updates using doc

Partial updates can be done using the `doc` parameter instead of `body`, where `doc` is a dictionary object that holds the partial fields that are to be updated. This is the preferable method to do partial updates. It can be done as shown in the following example:

```
es.update(index=index_name, doc_type=doc_type, 'doc': {'new_field':
'doing partial update with a new field'}, id='1', ignore=404)
```

> In most cases, where many documents need to be updated, document re-indexing makes more sense than updating it through a script or with `doc`.

Checking document existence

If it is required to check whether a document exists, you can use the `exists` function that returns either `true` or `false` in its response:

```
es.exists(index=index_name, doc_type=doc_type, id='1'):
```

Deleting a document

Document deletion can be done using the `delete` function in the following way:

```
es.delete(index=index_name, doc_type=doc_type, id='1', ignore=404)
```

CRUD operations using Java

In this section, we will go through the Elasticsearch Java client to perform the CRUD operations. To use a Java client of Elasticsearch, you can either build a Maven project (recommended) or simply add Elasticsearch jar files, which ship with the Elasticsearch installation file, into your project classpath.

You can include an Elasticsearch dependency in your Maven project by adding the following code to the project's pom.xml file:

```
<dependency>
    <groupId>org.elasticsearch</groupId>
    <artifactId>elasticsearch</artifactId>
    <version>2.0.0</version>
</dependency>
```

Connecting with Elasticsearch

To connect with Elasticsearch using its transport client, you need to add the following imports:

```
import org.elasticsearch.client.Client;
import org.elasticsearch.client.transport.TransportClient;
import org.elasticsearch.common.settings.Settings;
import org.elasticsearch.common.transport.InetSocketTransportAddress;
```

After this, a connection can be created with the following code snippet:

```
static Client client;
static Settings settings;
public static Client getEsConnection()
  {
  settings = Settings.settingsBuilder().put("cluster.name",
"elasticsearch").put("path.home", "/").put("client.transport.ping_
timeout","10s").build();
  try {
    client = TransportClient.builder().settings(settings)
          .addTransportAddress(new InetSocketTransportAddress(InetAddr
ess.getByName("localhost"), 9300));
  } catch (UnknownHostException e) {
    e.printStackTrace();
  }
  return client;
  }
```

To connect with more than one node of a single cluster, you can add more transport addresses in this way:

```
client = TransportClient.builder().settings(settings).build()
        .addTransportAddress(new InetSocketTransportAddress(InetAddr
ess.getByName("localhost"), 9300))
.addTransportAddress(new InetSocketTransportAddress(InetAddress.
getByName("some_other_host"), 9300));
```

Note that to create a connection with Elasticsearch using Java API, you need to first create settings by specifying the cluster name and can optionally provide a timeout that defaults to 5s.

This setting is then used by the transport client to create a connection with the Elasticsearch cluster over the TCP port 9300.

Indexing a document

To index a single document at once (sequential indexing), you can create documents in multiple ways, such as using plain JSON strings, or using Jackson API or your familiar HashMap. The following example shows the use of HashMap to create a document:

1. The first import will be as follows:

   ```
   import org.elasticsearch.action.index.IndexResponse;
   ```

2. Then create the document:

   ```
   Map<String, Object> document1= new HashMap<String, Object>();
       document1.put("screen_name", "d_bharvi");
       document1.put("followers_count", 2000);
       document1.put("create_at", "2015-09-20");
   ```

3. The preceding document can be indexed with the following code, assuming you have an object of the client available in your code:

   ```
   IndexResponse response = client.prepareIndex()
       .setIndex("IndexName").setType("docType")
       .setId("1").setSource(document1)
       .execute().actionGet();
   ```

   In the preceding code, the setIndex and setType methods take the index name and the name of the document type correspondingly.

   ○ The setSource method takes the actual data for indexing.

   ○ The setId method takes the unique document identifier. This is optional; Elasticsearch will generate it dynamically if it is not set.

There are many other methods available, which will see in the upcoming chapter.

Fetching a document

To fetch a document from Elasticsearch, you need its document ID. Once you know the document ID, it is simple to fetch it. Just add the following import:

```
import org.elasticsearch.action.get.GetResponse;
```

Then, you can get the document using `prepareGet`:

```
GetResponse response = client.prepareGet()
    .setIndex(indexName).setType(docType)
    .setId("1").execute().actionGet();
```

Updating a document

As you are aware, documents can be updated in two ways; first using `doc`, and the other way is to use script. In both cases, you need to import `UpdateResponse` to you, code:

```
import org.elasticsearch.action.delete.UpdateResponse;
```

Updating a document using doc

To do a partial update, you can create the object to be appended or replace an existing value for a field:

```
Map<String, Object> partialDoc1= new HashMap<String, Object>();
partialDoc1.put("user_name", "Bharvi Dixit");
```

Then, you can send it to Elasticsearch using the `prepareUpdate` method by setting the partial document inside the `setDoc` method:

```
UpdateResponse response = client.prepareUpdate()
    .setIndex(indexName).setType(docType)
    .setId("1").setDoc(partialDoc1)
    .execute().actionGet();
```

Updating a document using script

To use scripts for updating, first you need to make sure that you have enabled dynamic scripting in your `elasticsearch.yml` file. Then, you need to import the following classes into your code:

```
import org.elasticsearch.script.Script;
import org.elasticsearch.script.ScriptService.ScriptType;
```

Once the import is done, you can do the update in the following way:

```
String script = "ctx._source.user_name = \"Alberto Paro\"";
UpdateResponse response = client.prepareUpdate()
  .setIndex(indexName).setType(docType)
  .setScript(new Script(script, ScriptType.INLINE, "groovy", null)).
setId("1").execute().actionGet();
```

Note that in this example, the INLINE scripts have been used. You can also use file scripts or indexed scripts . You can find more about scripting here: `https://www.elastic.co/guide/en/elasticsearch/reference/2.0/modules-scripting.html`.

Deleting documents

To delete a single document in a single request, import the following line of code:

```
import org.elasticsearch.action.delete.DeleteResponse;
```

You can delete the document with the `prepareDelete` method using the document ID:

```
DeleteResponse response = client.prepareDelete()
      .setIndex(indexName).setType(docType)
      .setId("1").execute().actionGet();
```

Creating a search database

It's always good to have some practical examples with real data sets, and what could be better than real-time social media data? In this section, we will write the code that will fetch tweets from Twitter in real time based on the search keywords provided. There are three dependencies of the code written in this section:

- `tweepy` is a Python client for Twitter.
- `elasticsearch` is a Python client for Elasticsearch that we have already installed.
- For Twitter API access token keys, please follow the instructions at this link. `https://dev.twitter.com/oauth/overview/application-owner-access-tokens`, to create a sample Twitter application and get all the four keys that are needed to interact with the Twitter API. These four tokens are named: **Access Token**, **Access Token Secret**, **Consumer Key**, and **Consumer Secret**.

After generating the `auth` tokens and keys stored it inside `config.py` with the variable names: `consumer_key`, `consumer_secret`, `access_token`, and `access_token_secret`. The next step is to install `tweepy` using this command:

pip install tweepy

 If you get any error during the installation of `tweepy`, the version of `pip` may need to be upgraded. To upgrade the `pip` version use the following command: `pip install 'pip>1.5' --upgrade`.

It's good to do some hands-on while creating mappings. For this, first you need to understand the JSON data of Twitter. You can view a sample on the following URL and accordingly create mappings with the appropriate field types and analyzers: `https://gist.github.com/bharvidixit/0d35b7ac907127860e58`.

Once the mapping is created, write the code to start fetching tweets and indexing them in our index with the name `twitter`, and type `tweet`:

```
from tweepy import OAuthHandler
from tweepy import Stream
from tweepy.streaming import StreamListener
from elasticsearch import Elasticsearch
import config
import json

es = Elasticsearch('localhost:9200')

class StdOutListener(StreamListener):
    """A listener handles tweets that are received from the stream.
    This listener dumps the tweets into elasticsearch
    """
    counter = 0
    total_docs_to_be_indexed = 10000

def on_data(self, data):
        print data
        while self.total_docs_to_be_indexed > self.counter:

            tweet = json.loads(data)
            self.index_tweet(tweet)
            self.counter += 1
            return True

def index_tweet(self, tweet):
```

```
        es.index(index='twitter', doc_type='tweets',id=tweet['id_str'],
body=tweet)

def on_error(self, status):
        print status
    pass


#code execution starts here
if __name__ == '__main__':
    listener = StdOutListener()
    auth = OAuthHandler(config.consumer_key, config.consumer_secret)
    auth.set_access_token(config.access_token, config.access_token_
secret)
    stream = Stream(auth, listener)
#set the terms for tracking and fetching tweets from Twitter

    stream.filter(track=['crime', 'blast', 'earthquake', 'riot',
'politics'])
```

Elasticsearch Query-DSL

Query-DSL is a JSON interface provided by Elasticsearch to write queries in the JSON format. It allows you to write any query that you may write in Lucene. The queries can be as simple as just matching simple terms, or they can be very complex.

Until now, to retrieve documents from Elasticsearch we used a GET request that was dependent on the ID to search and retrieve the document. You can extend the searches in similar way; for example: `localhost:9200/index_name/doc_type/_search?q=category:databases`.

The preceding query is a typical Lucene `query string` that searches for the `databases` word inside the `category` field. Submitting queries to Elasticsearch in this way is very limited, so you will learn about Query-DSL now.

Syntax:

The Query-DSL follows the following syntax:

```
{
  "query": {},
  "from": 0,
  "size": 20,
  "_source": ["field1","field2"]
}
```

Understanding Query-DSL parameters

- `query`: The `query` object contains all the queries that need to be passed to Elasticsearch. For example, the query to find all the documents that belong to a search category can written as follows:

```
GET index_name/doc_type/_search
{
  "query": {
    "query_string": {
 "default_field": "category",
      "query": "search"
    }
  }
}
```

- `from` and `size`: These parameters control the pagination and the result size to be returned after querying. The `from` parameter is used to specify the starting point from which document the results will be returned. It defaults to `0`. The `size` parameter, which defaults to `10`, specifies how many top documents will be returned from the total matched documents in a corpus.

- `_source`: This is an optional parameter that takes field names in an array format, which are to be returned in the query results. It by default returns all the fields stored inside the `_source` field. If you do not want to return any field, you can specify `_source: false`.

Elasticsearch queries majorly fall into two categories:

- **Basic Queries**: These queries include normal keyword searching inside indexes.

- **Compound Queries**: These queries combine multiple basic queries together with Boolean clauses.

 We will be using our Twitter dataset to perform all the queries in this and the upcoming chapters.

Query types

At the abstract level, there are two major categories of queries in Elasticsearch:

- **Full-Text Search Queries**: These are the queries that usually run over text fields like a tweet text. These queries understand the field mapping, and depending on the field type and analyzer used for that field and query, the text goes through an analysis phase (similar to indexing) to find the relevant documents.

- **Term-based search queries**: Unlike full-text queries, term-based queries do not go through an analysis process. These queries are used to match the exact terms stored inside an inverted index.

> There exist a few other categories of queries such as **Compound Queries, Geo Queries**, and **Relational Queries**. We will cover **Compound Queries** in this chapter and the rest will be covered in the subsequent chapters.

Full-text search queries

The most important queries in this category are the following:

- `match_all`
- `match`
- `match_phrase`
- `multi_match`
- `query_string`

match_all

The simplest query in Elasticsearch is `match_all` query that matches all the documents. It gives a generous `_score` of `1.0` to each document in the index. The syntax of the `match_all` query is as follows:

```
{
    "query": {
        "match_all": {}
    }
}
```

match query

The text passed inside a match query goes through the analysis phase and, depending on the operator (which defaults to OR), documents are matched. For example:

```
{
    "query": {
        "match": {
            "text": "Build Great Web Apps",
            "operator" : "and"
        }
    }
}
```

The preceding query will match the documents that contain the Build, Great, Web, and Apps terms in the text field. If we had used the OR operator, it would have matched the documents containing any of these terms.

> If you want the exact matches, you need to pass the text in the following way so that the text is not broken into tokens:
>
> ```
> {
>     "query": {
>         "match": {
>             "text": "\"Build Great Web Apps\""
>         }
>     }
> }
> ```
>
> The preceding query will match the documents in which Build Great Web Apps appear together exactly in the same order.

Phrase search

Match query provides an option to search phrases with the type parameter in the following way:

```
{
    "query": {
        "match": {
            "text": "Build Great Web Apps",
            "type" : "phrase"
        }
    }
}
```

multi match

The `multi_match` query is similar to the `match` query but it provides options to search the same terms in more than one field at one go. For example:

```
{
  "query": {
  "multi_match": {
    "query": "Build Great Web Apps",
    "fields": ["text","retweeted_status.text"]
  }
  }
}
```

The preceding query will search the words `Build`, `Great`, `Web`, and `Apps` inside the two fields `text` and `retweeted_status.text`, and will return the relevant results in a sorted order based on the score each document gets. If you want to match only those documents in which all the terms are present, then use the `and` keyword in the `operator` parameter.

query_string

In comparison to all the other queries available in Elasticsearch, the `query_string` query provides a full Lucene syntax to be used in it. It uses a query parser to construct an actual query out of the provided text. Similar to the `match` query, it also goes through the analysis phase. The following is the syntax for `query_string`:

```
{
  "query": {
    "query_string": {
      "default_field": "text",
      "query": "text:analytics^2 +text:data -user.name:d_bharvi"
    }
  }
}
```

The `match` query that we used in the previous section can be written using a query string in the following way:

```
{
  "query": {
    "query_string": {
      "default_field": "text",
      "query": "Build Great Web Apps"
    }
  }
}
```

Term-based search queries

The most important queries in this category are the following:

- Term query
- Terms query
- Range query
- Exists query
- Missing query

Term query

The `term` query does an exact term matching in a given field. So, you need to provide the exact term to get the correct results. For example, if you have used a lowercase filter while indexing, you need to pass the terms in lowercase while querying with the `term` query.

The syntax for a `term` query is as follows:

```
{
    "query": {
        "term": {
            "text": "elasticsearch"
        }
    }
}
```

Terms query

If you want to search more than one term in a single field, you can use the `terms` query. For example, to search all the tweets in which the hashtags used are either `bomb` or `blast`, you can write a query like this:

```
{
    "query": {
        "terms": {
            "entities.hashtags": [
                "bomb",
                "blast"
            ],
            "minimum_match": 1
        }
    }
}
```

The `minimum_match` specifies the number of minimum terms that should match in each document. This parameter is optional.

Range queries

Range queries are used to find data within a certain range. The syntax of a `range` query is as follows and is the same for date fields as well as number fields such as `integer`, `long`, and so on:

```
{
    "query": {
        "range": {
            "user.followers_count": {
                "gte": 100,
                "lte": 200
            }
        }
    }
}
```

The preceding query will find all the tweets created by users whose follower count is between 100 and 200. The parameters supported in the range queries are: `gt`, `lt`, `gte`, and `lte`.

 Please note that if you use `range` queries on string fields, you will get weird results as strings. String ranges are calculated lexicographically or alphabetically, so a string stored as 50 will be lesser than 6. In addition, doing `range` queries on strings is a heavier operation in comparison to numbers.

Range queries on dates allow date math operations. So, for example, if you want to find all the tweets from the last one hour, you can use the following query:

```
{
    "query": {
        "range": {
            "created_at": {
                "gt": "now-1h"
            }
        }
    }
}
```

Similarly, months (M), minutes (m), years (y), and seconds (s) are allowed in the query.

Exists queries

The `exists` query matches documents that have at least one non-value in a given field. For example, the following query will find all the tweets that are replies to any other tweet:

```
{
  "query":{
    "constant_score":{
      "filter":{
        "exists":{"field":"in_reply_to_user_id"}
      }
    }
  }
}
```

Missing queries

`Missing` queries are the opposite of `exists` queries. They are used to find the documents that contain null values. For instance, the following query finds all the tweets that do not contain any hashtags:

```
{
  "query":{
    "constant_score":{
      "filter":{
        "missing":{"field":"hashtags"}
      }
    }
  }
}
```

The story of filters

Before version 2.0.0, Elasticsearch used to have two different objects for querying data: **Queries** and **Filters**. Both used to differ in functionality and performance.

Queries were used to find out how relevant a document was to a particular query by calculating a score for each document, whereas filters were used to match certain criteria and were cacheable to enable faster execution. This means that if a filter matched 1,000 documents, with the help of bloom filters, Elasticsearch used to cache them in the memory to get them quickly in case the same filter was executed again.

However, with the release of Lucene 5.0, which is used by Elasticsearch version 2.0.0, things have completely changed and both the queries and filters are now the same internal object. Users need not worry about caching and performance anymore, as Elasticsearch will take care of it. However, one must be aware of the contextual difference between a query and a filter that was listed in the previous paragraph.

In the query context, put the queries that ask the questions about document relevance and score calculations, while in the filter context, put the queries that need to match a simple yes/no question.

If you have been using an Elasticsearch version below 2.0.0, please go through the breaking changes here: `https://www.elastic.co/guide/en/elasticsearch/reference/2.0/breaking-changes-2.0.html`, and migrate your application code accordingly since there have been a lot of changes, including the removal of various filters.

Compound queries

Compound queries are offered by Elasticsearch to connect multiple simple queries together to make your search better. A compound query clause can combine any number of queries including compound ones that allow you to write very complex logic for your searches. You will need them at every step while creating any search application.

In the previous chapter, we saw how Lucene calculates a score based on the TF/IDF formula. This score is calculated for each and every query we send to Elasticsearch. Thus, when we combine queries in a compound form, the scores of all the queries are combined to calculate the overall score of the document.

The primary compound queries are as follows:

- `Bool` query
- `Not` query
- `Function score` query (will be discussed in *Chapter 8, Controlling Relevancy*)

Bool queries

`Bool` queries allow us to wrap up many queries clauses together including `bool` clauses. The documents are matched based on the combinations of these Boolean clauses that are listed as follows:

- `must`: The queries that are written inside this clause must match in order to return the documents.
- `should`: The queries written inside the `should` clause may or may not have a match but if the `bool` query has no `must` clause inside it, then at least one `should` condition needs to be matched in order to return the documents.
- `must_not`: The queries wrapped inside this clause must not appear in the matching documents.
- `filter`: A query wrapped inside this clause must appear in the matching documents. However, this does not contribute to scoring. The structure of `bool` queries is as follows:

```
{
  "query":{
  "bool":{
    "must":[{}],
    "should":[{}],
    "must_not":[{}]
    "filter":[{}]
    }
  }
}
```

There are some additional parameters supported by bool queries that are listed here:

- `boost`: This parameter controls the score of each query, which is wrapped inside the `must` or `should` clause.
- `minimum_should_match`: This is only used for the `should` clauses. Using this, we can specify how many `should` clauses must match in order to return a document.

- `disable_coord`: The bool queries by default use query coordination for all the `should` clauses; it is a good thing to have since the more clauses get matched, the higher the score a document will get. However, look at the following example where we may need to disable this:

```
{
"query":{
  "bool":{
    "disable_coord":true,
    "should":[
      {"term":{"text":{"value":"turmoil"}}},
      {"term":{"text":{"value":"riot"}}}
      ]
    }
  }
}
```

In the preceding example, inside the text field, we are looking for the terms `turmoil` and `riot`, which are synonyms of each other. In these cases, we do not care how many synonyms are present in the document since all have the same meaning. In these kinds of scenarios, we can disable query coordination by setting `disable_coord` to `true`, so that similar clauses do not impact the score factor computation.

Not queries

The `not` query is used to filter out the documents that match the query. For example, we can use the following to get the tweets that are not created within a certain range of time:

```
{
  "filter": {
    "not": {
      "filter": {
        "range": {
          "created_at": {
            "from": "2015-10-01",
            "to": "2010-10-30"
          }
        }
      }
    }
  }
}
```

Please note that any filter can be used inside bool queries with the `must`, `must_not`, or `should` blocks.

Search requests using Python

All the queries that we have discussed can be performed with the Elasticsearch Python client using the search function. To do this, first store the query inside a variable that is query in the following example:

```
query = {
    "query": {
        "match_all": {}
    },
}
```

Call the search function with all the parameters including the index name, document type, and query. The size parameter used in the following search request can also be included inside the query itself:

```
response = es.search(index='twitter', doc_type='tweets', body=query,
size=2, request_timeout=20)
```

 To search against more than one index, instead of using a string value, you need to use a list of index names. The same applies for document types too.

The response data comes in the following format:

```
{
  "hits": {
    "hits": [
      {
        "_score": 1,
        "_type": "tweets",
        "_id": "649956033515773953",
        "_source": {
          "contributors": null,
          "truncated": false,
          "text": "RT @lexcanroar: \"No mass shootings in the past 30
years have been stopped by an armed civilian.\""



      },
    {
    ...
```

```
    }
      "_index": "twitter"
     }
   ],
   "total": 124,
   "max_score": 1
 },
 "_shards": {
   "successful": 5,
   "failed": 0,
   "total": 5
 },
 "took": 5,
 "timed_out": false
}
```

The response contains an object hit that has an array of hits containing all the documents. Further, each hit inside an array of hits contains the following fields in it:

- _score: The document score with respect to the query
- _index: The index name to which the document belongs
- _type: The document type to which the document belongs
- _id: The unique ID of the document
- _source: This contains all the fields and values

The documents inside _source can be accessed with the following code:

```
for hit in response['hits']['hits']:
        print hit.get('_source')
```

Search requests using Java

While it's easy to write a JSON query and directly use it with the Python client, using Java client requires a bit of expertise to create queries using Elasticsearch Java APIs.

In Java, there is the QueryBuilder class that helps you in constructing queries. Once the queries are created, you can execute that query with the client's prepareSearch method.

First of all, you need the following imports in your code:

```
import org.elasticsearch.index.query.QueryBuilder;
import org.elasticsearch.index.query.QueryBuilders;
import org.elasticsearch.search.SearchHit;
```

Then you can start building queries and executing them:

```
QueryBuilder query = QueryBuilders.termQuery("screen_name", "d_
bharvi");
SearchResponse response = client.prepareSearch()
    .setIndices(indexName).setTypes(docType)
    .setQuery(query).setFrom(0).setSize(10)
    .execute().actionGet();
```

The preceding code shows an example of creating term queries where we search for a term, d_bharvi, inside the screen_name field.

Similarly, you can create all types of query against the QueryBuilders class. To take another example, a match_all query can be created by this:

```
QueryBuilders.matchAllQuery();
```

The other parameters are as follows:

- setIndices: This is required as search requests support a single search query to be executed against more than one index. You can specify comma-separated index names if you want to do so.

- setTypes: Similar to searching inside more than one index, a search can be executed inside more than one document type. Here, you can provide comma-separated type names if needed.

- setQuery: This method takes the actual query built using QueryBuilder.

- setFrom and setSize: These parameters are used for pagination purposes and to specify the number of documents that need to be returned.

Parsing search responses

A search response contains multiple document hits inside it that can be iterated by converting the response hits into a SearchHit array:

```
SearchHit[] results = response.getHits().getHits();
        for (SearchHit hit : results) {
            System.out.println(hit.getSource());
            //process documents
        }
```

There are many other methods supported for search requests. A full list can be found at this gist: https://gist.github.com/bharvidixit/357367e30cea59bb5d62.

Sorting your data

Data in Elasticsearch is by default sorted by a relevance score, which is computed using the Lucene scoring formula, TF/IDF. This relevance score is a floating point value that is returned with search results inside the _score parameter. By default, results are sorted in descending order.

> Sorting on nested and geo-points fields will be covered in the upcoming chapters.

See the following query for an example:

```
{
   "query": {
      "match": {
         "text": "data analytics"
      }
   }
}
```

We are searching for tweets that contain the data or analytics terms in their text fields. In some cases, however, we do not want the results to be sorted based on _score. Elasticsearch provides a way to sort documents in various ways. Let's explore how this can be done.

Sorting documents by field values

This section covers the sorting of documents based on the fields that contain a single value such as created_at, or followers_count. Please note that we are not talking about sorting string-based fields here.

Suppose we want to sort tweets that contain data or analytics in their text field based on their creation time in ascending order:

```
{
   "query":{
      "match":{"text":"data analytics"}
   },
   "sort":[
      {"created_at":{"order":"asc"}}
      ]
}
```

In the response of the preceding query, `max_score` and `_score` will have null as values. They are not calculated because `_score` is not used for sorting. You will see an additional field, `sort`. This field contains the date value in the long format, which has been used for sorting.

Sorting on more than one field

In scenarios where it is required to sort documents based on more than one field, one can use the following syntax for sorting:

```
"sort": [
{"created_at":{"order":"asc"},"followers_count":{"order":"asc"}}
]
```

With the above query, the results will be sorted first using tweet creation time, and if two tweets have the same tweet creation time, then they will be sorted using the followers count.

Sorting multivalued fields

Multivalued fields such as arrays of dates contain more than one value, and you cannot specify on which value to sort. So in this case, the single value needs to be calculated first using `mode` parameter that takes `min`, `max`, `avg`, `median`, or `sum` as a value. For example, in the following query the sorting will be done on the maximum value inside the `price` field of each document:

```
"sort" : [
     {"price" : {"order" : "asc", "mode" : "max"}}
  ]
```

Sorting on string fields

The `analyzed` string fields are also multivalued fields since they contain multiple tokens and because of performance considerations; do not use sorting on analyzed fields.

The string field on which sorting is to be done must be `not_analyzed` or keyword tokenized so that the field contains only one single token.

Sorting is an expensive process. All the values for the field on which sorting is to be performed are loaded into memory. So, you should have an ample amount of memory on the node to perform sorting. The data type of the field should also be chosen carefully while creating mapping. For example, short can be used in place of integer or long if the value is not going to be bigger.

Document routing

Document routing is the concept of indexing a document to a particular shard. By default, Elasticsearch tries to evenly distribute the documents among all the shards in an index. For this, it uses the following formula:

shard = hash(routing) % number_of_primary_shards

Here, shard is the shard number in which the document will be indexed and routing is the _id of a document.

We can explicitly specify the routing value while indexing, updating, fetching, or searching data in Elasticsearch. Custom routing yields faster indexing as well as faster searches. However, it is more about designing for scale that we will study in the following chapters.

Summary

In this chapter, you learned how to use Python and Java clients for Elasticsearch and perform CRUD operations using it. We also covered Elasticsearch Query-DSL, various queries, and data sorting techniques in this chapter.

In the next chapter, we will take a deep dive into the Elasticsearch aggregation framework.

4
Aggregations for Analytics

Elasticsearch is a search engine at the core but what makes it more usable is its ability to make complex data analytics in an easy and simple way. The volume of data is growing rapidly and companies want to perform analysis on data in real time. Whether it is log, real-time streaming of data, or static data, Elasticsearch works wonderfully in getting a summarization of data through its aggregation capabilities.

In this chapter, we will cover the following topics:

- Introducing the aggregation framework
- Metric and bucket aggregations
- Combining search, buckets, and metrics
- Memory pressure and implications

Introducing the aggregation framework

The aggregation functionality is completely different from search and enables you to ask sophisticated questions of the data. The use cases of aggregation vary from building analytical reports to getting real-time analysis of data and taking quick actions.

Also, despite being different in functionality, aggregations can operate along the usual search requests. Therefore, you can search or filter your data, and at the same time, you can also perform aggregation on the same datasets matched by search/filter criteria in a single request. A simple example can be to *find the maximum number of hashtags used by users related to tweets that has crime in the text field*. Aggregations enable you to calculate and summarize data about the current query on the fly. They can be used for all sorts of tasks such as dynamic counting of result values to building a histogram.

Aggregations come in two flavors: **metrics** and **buckets**.

- **Metrics**: Metrics are used to do statistics calculations, such as min, max, average, on a field of a document that falls into a certain criteria. An example of a metric can be to find the maximum count of followers among the user's follower counts.

- **Buckets**: Buckets are simply the grouping of documents that meet a certain criteria. They are used to categorize documents, for example:
    - The category of loans can fall into the buckets of home loan or personal loan
    - The category of an employee can be either male or female

Elasticsearch offers a wide variety of buckets to categorize documents in many ways such as by days, age range, popular terms, or locations. However, all of them work on the same principle: **document categorization based on some criteria**.

The most interesting part is that bucket aggregations can be nested within each other. This means that a bucket can contain other buckets within it. Since each of the buckets defines a set of documents, one can create another aggregation on that bucket, which will be executed in the context of its parent bucket. For example, a country-wise bucket can include a state-wise bucket, which can further include a city-wise bucket.

> In SQL terms, metrics are simply functions such as MIN(), MAX(), SUM(), COUNT(), and AVG(), where buckets group the results using GROUP BY queries.

Aggregation syntax

Aggregation follows the following syntax:

```
"aggregations" : {
    "<aggregation_name>" : {
        "<aggregation_type>" : {
            <aggregation_body>
        }
        [,"aggregations" : { [<sub_aggregation>]+ } ]?
    }
    [,"<aggregation_name_2>" : { ... } ]*
}
```

Let's understand how the preceding structure works:

- **aggregations**: The aggregations objects (which can also be replaced with `agg`) in the preceding structure holds the aggregations that have to be computed. There can be more than one aggregation inside this object.

- **<aggregation_name>**: This is a user-defined logical name for the aggregations that are held by the aggregations object (for example, if you want to compute the average age of users in the index, it makes sense to give the name as `avg_age`). These logical names will also be used to uniquely identify the aggregations in the response.

- **<aggregation_type>**: Each aggregation has a specific type, for example, `terms`, `sum`, `avg`, `min`, and so on.

- **<aggregation_body>**: Each type of aggregation defines its own body depending on the nature of the aggregation (for example, an `avg` aggregation on a specific field will define the field on which the average will be calculated).

- **<sub_aggregation>**: The sub aggregations are defined on the bucketing aggregation level and are computed for all the buckets built by the bucket aggregation. For example, if you define a set of aggregations under the range aggregation, the sub aggregations will be computed for the range buckets that are defined.

Look at the following JSON structure to understand a more simple structure of aggregations:

```
{
  "aggs": {
    "NAME1": {
      "AGG_TYPE": {},
      "aggs": {
        "NAME": {
          "AGG_TYPE": {}
        }
      }
    },
    "NAME2": {
      "AGG_TYPE": {}
    }
  }
}
```

Extracting values

Aggregations typically work on the values extracted from the aggregated document set. These values can be extracted either from a specific field using the field key inside the aggregation body or can also be extracted using a script.

While it's easy to define a field to be used to aggregate data, the syntax of using scripts needs some special understanding. The benefit of using scripts is that one can combine the values from more than one field to use as a single value inside an aggregation.

 Using scripting requires much more computation power and slows down the performance on bigger datasets.

The following are the examples of extracting values from a script:

Extracting a value from a single field:

```
{ "script" : "doc['field_name'].value" }
```

Extracting and combining values from more than one field:

```
"script": "doc['author.first_name'].value + ' ' +
doc['author.last_name'].value"
```

The scripts also support the use of parameters using the `param` keyword. For example:

```
{
  "avg": {
    "field": "price",
    "script": {
      "inline": "_value * correction",
      "params": {
        "correction": 1.5
      }
    }
  }
}
```

The preceding aggregation calculates the average price after multiplying each value of the price field with `1.5`, which is used as an inline function parameter.

Returning only aggregation results

Elasticsearch by default computes aggregations on a complete set of documents using the `match_all` query and returns 10 documents by default along with the output of the aggregation results.

If you do not want to include the documents in the response, you need to set the value of the size parameter to 0 inside your query. Note that you do not need to use the from parameter in this case. This is a very useful parameter because it avoids document relevancy calculation and the inclusion of documents in the response, and only returns the aggregated data.

Metric aggregations

As explained in the previous sections, metric aggregations allow you to find out the statistical measurement of the data, which includes the following:

- Computing basic statistics
    - Computing in a combined way: `stats` aggregation
    - Computing separately : `min`, `max`, `sum`, `value_count`, aggregations
- Computing extended statistics: `extended_stats` aggregation
- Computing distinct counts: `cardinality` aggregation

> Metric aggregations are fundamentally categorized in two forms:
>
> - **single-value metric**: `min`, `max`, `sum`, `value_count`, `avg`, and `cardinality` aggregations
> - **multi-value metric**: `stats` and `extended_stats` aggregations

Computing basic stats

The basic statistics include: min, max, sum, count, and avg. These statistics can be computed in the following two ways and can only be performed on numeric fields.

Combined stats

All the stats mentioned previously can be calculated with a single aggregation query.

Python example

```python
query = {
  "aggs": {
    "follower_counts_stats": {
      "stats": {
        "field": "user.followers_count"
      }
    }
  }
}
res = es.search(index='twitter', doc_type='tweets', body=query)
print resp
```

The response would be as follows:

```
"aggregations": {
    "follower_counts_stats": {
        "count": 124,
        "min": 2,
        "max": 38121,
        "avg": 2102.814516129032,
        "sum": 260749
    }
}
```

In the preceding response, count is the total values on which the aggregation is executed.

- min is the minimum follower count of a user
- max is the maximum follower count of a user
- avg is the average count of followers
- Sum is the addition of all the followers count

Java example

 In Java, all the metric aggregations can be created using the `MetricsAggregationBuilder` and `AggregationBuilders` classes. However, you need to import a specific package into your code to parse the results.

To build and execute a `stats` aggregation in Java, first do the following imports in the code:

```
import org.elasticsearch.search.aggregations.metrics.stats.Stats;
```

Then build the aggregation in the following way:

```
MetricsAggregationBuilder aggregation =
        AggregationBuilders
                .stats("follower_counts_stats")
                .field("user.followers_count");
```

This aggregation can be executed with the following code snippet:

```
SearchResponse response = client.prepareSearch(indexName).
setTypes(docType).setQuery(QueryBuilders.matchAllQuery())
    .addAggregation(aggregation)
    .execute().actionGet();
```

The `stats` aggregation response can be parsed as follows:

```
Stats agg = sr.getAggregations().get("follower_counts_stats");
long min = agg.getMin();
long max = agg.getMax();
double avg = agg.getAvg();
long sum = agg.getSum();
long count = agg.getCount();
```

Computing stats separately

In addition to computing these basic stats in a single query, Elasticsearch provides multiple aggregations to compute them one by one. The following are the aggregation types that fall into this category:

- `value_count`: This counts the number of values that are extracted from the aggregated documents

- `min`: This finds the minimum value among the numeric values extracted from the aggregated documents

- max: This finds the maximum value among the numeric values extracted from the aggregated documents
- avg: This finds the average value among the numeric values extracted from the aggregated documents
- sum: This finds the sum of all the numeric values extracted from the aggregated documents

To perform these aggregations, you just need to use the following syntax:

```
{
  "aggs": {
    "aggaregation_name": {
      "aggrigation_type": {
        "field": "name_of_the_field"
      }
    }
  }
}
```

Python example

```
query = {
  "aggs": {
    "follower_counts_stats": {
      "sum": {
        "field": "user.followers_count"
      }
    }
  },"size": 0
}
res = es.search(index='twitter', doc_type='tweets', body=query)
```

We used the sum aggregation type in the preceding query; for other aggregations such as min, max, avg, and value_count, just replace the type of aggregation in the query.

Java example

To perform these aggregations using the Java client, you need to follow this syntax:

```
MetricsAggregationBuilder aggregation =
        AggregationBuilders
                .sum("follower_counts_stats")
                .field("user.followers_count");
```

Note that in the preceding aggregation, instead of sum, you just need to call the corresponding aggregation type to build other types of metric aggregations such as, `min`, `max`, `count`, and `avg`. The rest of the syntax remains the same.

For parsing the responses, you need to import the correct package according to the aggregation type. The following are the imports that you will need:

- **For min aggregation**:

  ```
  import org.elasticsearch.search.aggregations.metrics.min.Min;
  ```

  The parsing response will be as follows:

  ```
  Min agg = response.getAggregations().get("follower_counts_stats");
  double value = agg.getValue();
  ```

- **For max aggregation**:

  ```
  import org.elasticsearch.search.aggregations.metrics.min.Max;
  ```

  The parsing response will be:

  ```
  Max agg = response.getAggregations().get("follower_counts_stats");
  double value = agg.getValue();
  ```

- **For avg aggregation**:

  ```
  import org.elasticsearch.search.aggregations.metrics.min.Avg;
  ```

  The parsing response will be this:

  ```
  Avg agg = response.getAggregations().get("follower_counts_stats");
  double value = agg.getValue();
  ```

- **For sum aggregation**:

  ```
  import org.elasticsearch.search.aggregations.metrics.min.Sum;
  ```

  This will be the parsing response:

  ```
  Sum agg = response.getAggregations().get("follower_counts_stats");
  double value = agg.getValue();
  ```

 Stats aggregations cannot contain sub aggregations. However, they can be a part of the sub aggregations of buckets.

Computing extended stats

The `extended_stats` aggregation is the extended version of `stats` aggregation and provides advanced statistics of the data, which include sum of square, variance, standard deviation, and standard deviation bounds.

So, if we hit the query with the `extended_stats` aggregation on the followers count field, we will get the following data:

```
"aggregations": {
    "follower_counts_stats": {
        "count": 124,
        "min": 2,
        "max": 38121,
        "avg": 2102.814516129032,
        "sum": 260749,
        "sum_of_squares": 3334927837,
        "variance": 22472750.441402186,
        "std_deviation": 4740.543264374051,
        "std_deviation_bounds": {
            "upper": 11583.901044877135,
            "lower": -7378.272012619071
        }
    }
}
```

Python example

```python
query = {
    "aggs": {
        "follower_counts_stats": {
            "extended_stats": {
                "field": "user.followers_count"
            }
        }
    }
}, "size": 0
res = es.search(index='twitter', doc_type='tweets', body=query)
```

Java example

An extended aggregation is build using the Java client in the following way:

```
MetricsAggregationBuilder aggregation =
        AggregationBuilders
                .extendedStats("agg_name")
                .field("user.follower_count");
```

To parse the response of the `extended_stats` aggregation in Java, you need to have the following `import` statement:

```
import org.elasticsearch.search.aggregations.metrics.stats.extended.
ExtendedStats;
```

Then the response can parsed in the following way:

```
ExtendedStats agg = response.getAggregations().get("agg_name");
double min = agg.getMin();
double max = agg.getMax();
double avg = agg.getAvg();
double sum = agg.getSum();
long count = agg.getCount();
double stdDeviation = agg.getStdDeviation();
double sumOfSquares = agg.getSumOfSquares();
double variance = agg.getVariance();
```

Finding distinct counts

The count of a distinct value of a field can be calculated using the cardinality aggregation. For example, we can use this to calculate unique users:

```
{
   "aggs": {
     "unique_users": {
       "cardinality": {
         "field": "user.screen_name"
       }
     }
   }
}
```

The response will be as follows:

```
"aggregations": {
    "unique_users": {
        "value": 122
    }
}
```

Java example

Cardinality aggregation is built using the Java client in the following way:

```
MetricsAggregationBuilder aggregation =
        AggregationBuilders
                .cardinality("unique_users")
                .field("user.screen_name");
```

To parse the response of the cardinality aggregation in Java, you need to have the following `import` statement:

```
import org.elasticsearch.search.aggregations.metrics.cardinality.
Cardinality;
```

Then the response can parsed in the following way:

```
Cardinality agg = response.getAggregations().get("unique_users");
long value = agg.getValue();
```

Bucket aggregations

Similar to metric aggregations, `bucket` aggregations are also categorized into two forms: **Single buckets** that contain only a single bucket in the response, and **multi buckets** that contain more than one bucket in the response.

The following are the most important aggregations that are used to create buckets:

- Multi bucket aggregations
    - Terms aggregation
    - Range aggregation
    - Date range aggregation
    - Histogram aggregation
    - Date histogram aggregation

- Single bucket aggregation

  ○ Filter-based aggregation

 We will cover a few more aggregations such as `nested` and `geo` aggregations in subsequent chapters.

`Buckets` aggregation response formats are different from the response formats of metric aggregations. The response of a `bucket` aggregation usually comes in the following format:

```
"aggregations": {

    "aggregation_name": {
        "buckets": [
            {
                "key": value,
                "doc_count": value
            },
            ......
        ]
    }
}
```

 All the bucket aggregations can be created in Java using the `AggregationBuilder` and `AggregationBuilders` classes. You need to have the following classes imported inside your code for the same:

> `org.elasticsearch.search.aggregations.`
> `AggregationBuilder;`
>
> `org.elasticsearch.search.aggregations.`
> `AggregationBuilders;`

Also, all the aggregation queries can be executed with the following code snippet:

> `SearchResponse response =    client.`
> `prepareSearch(indexName).setTypes(docType)`
>
> `.setQuery(QueryBuilders.matchAllQuery())`
>
> `.addAggregation(aggregation)`
>
> `.execute().actionGet();`

The `setQuery()` method can take any type of Elasticsearch query, whereas the `addAggregation()` method takes the aggregation built using `AggregationBuilder`.

Terms aggregation

Terms aggregation is the most widely used aggregation type and returns the buckets that are dynamically built using one per unique value.

Let's see how to find the top 10 hashtags used in our Twitter index in descending order.

Python example

```
query = {
  "aggs": {
    "top_hashtags": {
      "terms": {
        "field": "entities.hashtags.text",
        "size": 10,
        "order": {
          "_term": "desc"
        }
      }
    }
  }
}
```

In the preceding example, the size parameter controls how many buckets are to be returned (defaults to 10) and the order parameter controls the sorting of the bucket terms (defaults to asc):

```
res = es.search(index='twitter', doc_type='tweets', body=query)
```

The response would look like this:

```
"aggregations": {
    "top_hashtags": {
        "doc_count_error_upper_bound": 0,
        "sum_other_doc_count": 44,
        "buckets": [
            {
                "key": "politics",
                "doc_count": 2
            },
            ..............
        ]
    }
}
```

Java example

`Terms` aggregation can be built as follows:

```
AggregationBuilder aggregation =
        AggregationBuilders.terms("agg").field(fieldName)
        .size(10);
```

Here, `agg` is the aggregation bucket name and `fieldName` is the field on which the aggregation is performed.

The response object can be parsed as follows:

To parse the terms aggregation response, you need to import the following class:

```
import org.elasticsearch.search.aggregations.bucket.terms.Terms;
```

Then, the response can be parsed with the following code snippet:

```
Terms screen_names = response.getAggregations().get("agg");
    for (Terms.Bucket entry : screen_names.getBuckets()) {
        entry.getKey();        // Term
        entry.getDocCount(); // Doc count
    }
```

Range aggregation

With range aggregation, a user can specify a set of ranges, where each range represents a bucket. Elasticsearch will put the document sets into the correct buckets by extracting the value from each document and matching it against the specified ranges.

Python example

```
query = "aggs": {
  "status_count_ranges": {
    "range": {
      "field": "user.statuses_count",
      "ranges": [
        {
          "to": 50
        },
        {
          "from": 50,
          "to": 100
        }
```

```
            ]
          }
        }
      }
    },"size": 0
  }
  res = es.search(index='twitter', doc_type='tweets', body=query)
```

 The range aggregation always discards the *to* value for each range and only includes the from value.

The response for the preceding query request would look like this:

```
"aggregations": {
    "status_count_ranges": {
        "buckets": [
            {
                "key": "*-50.0",
                "to": 50,
                "to_as_string": "50.0",
                "doc_count": 3
            },
            {
                "key": "50.0-100.0",
                "from": 50,
                "from_as_string": "50.0",
                "to": 100,
                "to_as_string": "100.0",
                "doc_count": 3
            }
        ]
    }
}
```

Java example

Building range aggregation:

```
AggregationBuilder aggregation =
    AggregationBuilders
    .range("agg")
    .field(fieldName)
    .addUnboundedTo(1)      // from -infinity to 1 (excluded)
    .addRange(1, 100)   // from 1 to 100(excluded)
    .addUnboundedFrom(100); // from 100 to +infinity
```

Here, `agg` is the aggregation bucket name and `fieldName` is the field on which the aggregation is performed. The `addUnboundedTo` method is used when you do not specify the `from` parameter and the `addUnboundedFrom` method is used when you don't specify the `to` parameter.

Parsing the response

To parse the `range` aggregation response, you need to import the following class:

```
import org.elasticsearch.search.aggregations.bucket.range.Range;
```

Then, the response can be parsed with the following code snippet:

```
Range agg = response.getAggregations().get("agg");
for (Range.Bucket entry : agg.getBuckets()) {
    String key = entry.getKeyAsString();        // Range as key
    Number from = (Number) entry.getFrom();     // Bucket from
    Number to = (Number) entry.getTo();         // Bucket to
    long docCount = entry.getDocCount();        // Doc count
}
```

Date range aggregation

The `date range` aggregation is dedicated for date fields and is similar to range aggregation. The only difference between range and date range aggregation is that the latter allows you to use a `date math` expression inside the from and to fields. The following table shows an example of using math operations in Elasticsearch. The supported time units for the math operations are: y (year), M (month), w (week), d (day), h (hour), m (minute), and s (second):

Operation	Description
Now	Current time
Now+1h	Current time plus 1 hour
Now-1M	Current time minus 1 month
Now+1h+1m	Current time plus 1 hour plus one minute
Now+1h/d	Current time plus 1 hour rounded to the nearest day
2016-01-01||+1M/d	2016-01-01 plus 1 month rounded to the nearest day

Python example

```
query = {
        "aggs": {
          "tweets_creation_interval": {
```

```
            "range": {
              "field": "created_at",
              "format": "yyyy",
              "ranges": [
                {
                  "to": 2000
                },
                {
                  "from": 2000,
                  "to": 2005
                },
                {
                  "from": 2005
                }
              ]
            }
          }
        },"size": 0
    }
res = es.search(index='twitter', doc_type='tweets', body=query)
print res
```

Java example

Building date range aggregation:

```
AggregationBuilder aggregation =
  AggregationBuilders
  .dateRange("agg")
  .field(fieldName)
  .format("yyyy")
  .addUnboundedTo("2000")    // from -infinity to 2000 (excluded)
  .addRange("2000", "2005")  // from 2000 to 2005 (excluded)
  .addUnboundedFrom("2005"); // from 2005 to +infinity
```

Here, agg is the aggregation bucket name and fieldName is the field on which the aggregation is performed. The addUnboundedTo method is used when you do not specify the from parameter and the addUnboundedFrom method is used when you don't specify the to parameter.

Parsing the response:

To parse the date range aggregation response, you need to import the following class:

```
import org.elasticsearch.search.aggregations.bucket.range.Range;
import org.joda.time.DateTime;
```

Then, the response can be parsed with the following code snippet:

```
Range agg = response.getAggregations().get("agg");
for (Range.Bucket entry : agg.getBuckets()) {
   String key = entry.getKeyAsString();    // Date range as key
   DateTime fromAsDate = (DateTime) entry.getFrom(); // Date bucket
from as a Date
   DateTime toAsDate = (DateTime) entry.getTo(); // Date bucket to as a
Date
   long docCount = entry.getDocCount();            // Doc count
}
```

Histogram aggregation

A histogram aggregation works on numeric values extracted from documents and creates fixed-sized buckets based on those values. Let's see an example for creating buckets of a user's favorite tweet counts:

Python example

```
query = {
  "aggs": {
    "favorite_tweets": {
      "histogram": {
        "field": "user.favourites_count",
        "interval": 20000
      }
    }
  }, "size": 0
}
res = es.search(index='twitter', doc_type='tweets', body=query)
for bucket in res['aggregations']['favorite_tweets']['buckets']:
    print bucket['key'], bucket['doc_count']
```

The response for the preceding query will look like the following, which says that 114 users have favorite tweets between 0 to 20000 and 8 users have more than 20000 as their favorite tweets:

```
"aggregations": {
    "favorite_tweets": {
        "buckets": [
            {
                "key": 0,
                "doc_count": 114
            },
```

```
            {
                "key": 20000,
                "doc_count": 8
            }
        ]

    }

}
```

 While executing the histogram aggregation, the values of the documents are rounded off and they fall into the closest bucket; for example, if the favorite tweet count is 72 and the bucket size is set to 5, it will fall into the bucket with the key 70.

Java example

Building histogram aggregation:

```
AggregationBuilder aggregation =
        AggregationBuilders
        .histogram("agg")
        .field(fieldName)
        .interval(5);
```

Here, agg is the aggregation bucket name and fieldName is the field on which aggregation is performed. The interval method is used to pass the interval for generating the buckets.

Parsing the response:

To parse the histogram aggregation response, you need to import the following class:

```
import org.elasticsearch.search.aggregations.bucket.histogram.
Histogram;
```

Then, the response can be parsed with the following code snippet:

```
Range agg = response.getAggregations().get("agg");
for (Histogram.Bucket entry : agg.getBuckets()) {
    Long key = (Long) entry.getKey();        // Key
    long docCount = entry.getDocCount();     // Doc coun
}
```

Date histogram aggregation

Date histogram is similar to the `histogram` aggregation but it can only be applied to date fields. The difference between the two is that date histogram allows you to specify intervals using date/time expressions.

The following values can be used for intervals:

- year, quarter, month, week, day, hour, minute, and second

You can also specify fractional values, such as 1h (1 hour), 1m (1 minute) and so on.

Date histograms are mostly used to generate time-series graphs in many applications.

Python example

```
query = {
     "aggs": {
        "tweet_histogram": {
           "date_histogram": {
              "field": "created_at",
              "interval": "hour"
           }
        }
     }, "size": 0
   }
```

The preceding aggregation will generate an hourly-based tweet timeline on the field, created_at:

```
res = es.search(index='twitter', doc_type='tweets', body=query)
for bucket in res['aggregations']['tweet_histogram']['buckets']:
    print bucket['key'], bucket['key_as_string'], bucket['doc_count']
```

Java example

Building date histogram aggregation:

```
AggregationBuilder aggregation =
        AggregationBuilders
        .histogram("agg")
        .field(fieldName)
        .interval(DateHistogramInterval.YEAR);
```

Here, `agg` is the aggregation `bucket` name and `fieldname` is the field on which the aggregation is performed. The `interval` method is used to pass the interval to generate buckets. For interval in days, you can do this:

`DateHistogramInterval.days(10)`

Parsing the response:

To parse the `date histogram` aggregation response, you need to import the following class:

```
import org.elasticsearch.search.aggregations.bucket.histogram.
DateHistogramInterval;
```

The response can be parsed with this code snippet:

```
Histogram agg = response.getAggregations().get("agg");
for (Histogram.Bucket entry : agg.getBuckets()) {
  DateTime key = (DateTime) entry.getKey();      // Key
  String keyAsString = entry.getKeyAsString(); // Key as String
  long docCount = entry.getDocCount();         // Doc count
  }
```

Filter-based aggregation

Elasticsearch allows filters to be used as aggregations too. Filters preserve their behavior in the aggregation context as well and are usually used to narrow down the current aggregation context to a specific set of documents. You can use any filter such as `range`, `term`, `geo`, and so on.

To get the count of all the tweets done by the user, `d_bharvi`, use the following code:

Python example

```
query = {
  "aggs": {
    "screename_filter": {
      "filter": {
        "term": {
          "user.screen_name": "d_bharvi"
        }
      }
    }
  },"size": 0
}
```

In the preceding request, we have used a term filter to narrow down the bucket of tweets done by a particular user:

```
res = es.search(index='twitter', doc_type='tweets', body=query)
    for bucket in res['aggregations']['screename_filter']['buckets']:
        print bucket['doc_count']
```

The response would look like this:

```
"aggregations": {
    "screename_filter": {
        "doc_count": 100
    }
  }
}
```

Java example

Building filter-based aggregation:

```
AggregationBuilder aggregation =
  AggregationBuilders
  .filter("agg")
  .filter(QueryBuilders.termQuery("user.screen_name ", "d_bharvi"));
```

Here, agg is the aggregation bucket name under the first filter method and the second filter method takes a query to apply the filter.

Parsing the response:

To parse a filter-based aggregation response, you need to import the following class:

```
import org.elasticsearch.search.aggregations.bucket.histogram.
DateHistogramInterval;
```

The response can be parsed with the following code snippet:

```
Filter agg = response.getAggregations().get("agg");
    agg.getDocCount(); // Doc count
```

Combining search, buckets, and metrics

We can always combine searches, filters bucket aggregations, and metric aggregations
to get a more and more complex analysis. Until now, we have seen single levels of
aggregations; however, as explained in the aggregation syntax section earlier, an
aggregation can contain multiple levels of aggregations within. However, metric
aggregations cannot contain further aggregations within themselves. Also, when you
run an aggregation, it is executed on all the documents in the index for a document
type if specified on a match_all query context, but you can always use any type of
Elasticsearch query with an aggregation. Let's see how we can do this in Python and
Java clients.

Python example

```python
query = {
  "query": {
    "match": {
      "text": "crime"
    }
  },
  "aggs": {
    "hourly_timeline": {
      "date_histogram": {
        "field": "created_at",
        "interval": "hour"
      },
      "aggs": {
        "top_hashtags": {
          "terms": {
            "field": "entities.hashtags.text",
            "size": 1
          },
          "aggs": {
            "top_users": {
              "terms": {
                "field": "user.screen_name",
                "size": 1
              },
              "aggs": {
                "average_tweets": {
                  "avg": {
                    "field": "user.statuses_count"
                  }
                }
              }
```

```
                }
               }
              }
             }
            }
           }
          }
        } ,"size": 0
       }
      res = es.search(index='twitter', doc_type='tweets', body=query)
```

Parsing the response data:

```
for timeline_bucket in res['aggregations']['hourly_timeline']
['buckets']:
    print 'time range', timeline_bucket['key_as_string']
    print 'tweet count ',timeline_bucket['doc_count']
    for hashtag_bucket in timeline_bucket['top_hashtags']['buckets']:
        print 'hashtag key ', hashtag_bucket['key']
        print 'hashtag count ', hashtag_bucket['doc_count']
        for user_bucket in hashtag_bucket['top_users']['buckets']:
            print 'screen_name ', user_bucket['key']
            print 'count', user_bucket['doc_count']
            print 'average tweets', user_bucket['average_tweets']
['value']
```

And you will find the output as below:

```
time_range 2015-10-14T10:00:00.000Z
tweet_count   1563
  hashtag_key   crime
  hashtag_count   42
    screen_name   andresenior
    count 2
    average_tweets 9239.0

. . . . . . . . . . .
```

Understanding the response in the context of our search of the term crime in a text field:

- **time_range**: The key of the `daywise_timeline` bucket
- **tweet_count**: The number of tweets happening per hour
- **hashtag_key**: The name of the hashtag used by users within the specified time bucket

- **hashtag_count**: The count of each hashtag within the specified time bucket
- **screen_name**: The screen name of the user who has tweeted using that hashtag
- **count**: The number of times that user tweeted using a corresponding hashtag
- **average_tweets**: The average number of tweets done by users in their lifetime who have used this particular hashtag

Java example

Writing multilevel aggregation queries (as we just saw) in Java seems quite complex, but once you learn the basics of structuring aggregations, it becomes fun.

Let's see how we write the previous query in Java:

Building the query using QueryBuilder:

```
QueryBuilder query = QueryBuilders.matchQuery("text", "crime");
```

Building the aggregation:

The syntax for a multilevel aggregation in Java is as follows:

```
AggregationBuilders
        .aggType("aggs_name")
        //aggregation_definition
        .subAggregation(AggregationBuilders
            .aggType("aggs_name")
            //aggregation_definition
          .subAggregation(AggregationBuilders
            .aggType("aggs_name")
            //aggregation_definition........
```

You can relate the preceding syntax with the aggregation syntax you learned in the beginning of this chapter.

The exact aggregation for our Python example will be as follows:

```
AggregationBuilder aggregation =
        AggregationBuilders
        .dateHistogram("hourly_timeline")
        .field("@timestamp")
        .interval(DateHistogramInterval.YEAR)
        .subAggregation(AggregationBuilders
            .terms("top_hashtags")
            .field("entities.hashtags.text")
        .subAggregation(AggregationBuilders
```

```
      .terms("top_users")
      .field("user.screen_name")
   .subAggregation(AggregationBuilders
      .avg("average_status_count")
      .field("user.statuses_count")))));
```

Let's execute the request by combining the query and aggregation we have built:

```
SearchResponse response = client.prepareSearch(indexName).
setTypes(docType)
      .setQuery(query).addAggregation(aggregation)
      .setSize(0)
      .execute().actionGet();
```

Parsing multilevel aggregation responses:

Since multilevel aggregations are nested inside each other, you need to iterate accordingly to parse each level of aggregation response in loops.

The response for our request can be parsed with the following code:

```
//Get first level of aggregation data
Histogram agg = response.getAggregations().get("hourly_timeline");
//for each entry of hourly histogram
for (Histogram.Bucket entry : agg.getBuckets()) {
  DateTime key = (DateTime) entry.getKey();
  String keyAsString = entry.getKeyAsString();
  long docCount = entry.getDocCount();
  System.out.println(key);
  System.out.println(docCount);

  //Get second level of aggregation data
  Terms topHashtags = entry.getAggregations().get("top_hashtags");
  //for each entry of top hashtags
  for (Terms.Bucket hashTagEntry : topHashtags.getBuckets()) {
      String hashtag = hashTagEntry.getKey().toString();
      long hashtagCount = hashTagEntry.getDocCount();
System.out.println(hashtag);
      System.out.println(hashtagCount);

      //Get 3rd level of aggregation data
      Terms topUsers = hashTagEntry.getAggregations()
              .get("top_users");
      //for each entry of top users
      for (Terms.Bucket usersEntry : topUsers.getBuckets()) {
```

```
        String screenName = usersEntry.getKey().toString();
long userCount = usersEntry.getDocCount();                    System.out.
println(screenName);
        System.out.println(userCount);

        //Get 4th level of aggregation data
        Avg average_status_count = usersEntry
                    .getAggregations()
        .get("average_status_count");
        double max = average_status_count.getValue();
        System.out.println(max);
        }
    }
  }
}
```

As you saw, building these types of aggregations and going for a drill down on data sets to do complex analytics can be fun. However, one has to keep in mind the pressure on memory that Elasticsearch bears while doing these complex calculations. The next section covers how we can avoid these memory implications.

Memory pressure and implications

Aggregations are awesome! However, they bring a lot of memory pressure on Elasticsearch. They work on an in-memory data structure called **fielddata**, which is the biggest consumer of HEAP memory in a Elasticsearch cluster. Fielddata is not only used for aggregations, but also used for sorting and scripts. The in-memory fielddata is slow to load, as it has to read the whole inverted index and un-invert it. If the fielddata cache fills up, old data is evicted causing heap churn and bad performance (as fielddata is reloaded and evicted again.)

The more unique terms exist in the index, the more terms will be loaded into memory and the more pressure it will have. If you are using an Elasticsearch version below 2.0.0 and above 1.0.0, then you can use the doc_vlaues parameter inside the mapping while creating the index to avoid the use of fielddata using the following syntax:

```
PUT /index_name/_mapping/index_type
{
  "properties": {
    "field_name": {
      "type": "string",
      "index": "not_analyzed",
      "doc_values": true
    }
  }
}
```

`doc_values` have been enabled by default from Elasticsearch version 2.0.0 onwards.

The advantages of using `doc_values` are as follows:

- Less heap usage and faster garbage collections
- No longer limited by the amount of fielddata that can fit into a given amount of heap—instead the file system caches can make use of all the available RAM
- Fewer latency spikes caused by reloading a large segment into memory

The other important consideration to keep in mind is not to have a huge number of buckets in a nested aggregation. For example, finding the total order value for a country during a year with an interval of one week will generate 100*51 buckets with the sum value. It is a big overhead that is not only calculated in data nodes, but also in the co-ordinating node that aggregates them. A big JSON also gives problems on parsing and loading on the "frontend". It will easily kill a server with wide aggregations.

Summary

In this chapter, we learned about one of the most powerful features of Elasticsearch, that is, aggregation frameworks. We went through the most important metric and bucket aggregations along with examples of doing analytics on our Twitter dataset with Python and Java API.

This chapter covered many fundamental as well complex examples of the different facets of analytics, which can be built using a combination of full-text searches, term-based searches, and multilevel aggregations. Elasticsearch is awesome for analytics but one should always keep in mind the memory implications, which we covered in the last section of this chapter, to avoid the over killing of nodes.

In the next chapter, we will learn to work with geo spatial data in Elasticsearch and we will also cover analytics with `geo` aggregations.

5
Data Looks Better on Maps: Master Geo-Spatiality

The world is getting smarter day by day and searches based on locations have become an integral part of our daily life. Be it searching for shopping centers, hospitals, restaurants, or any locations, we always look out for information such as distance and other information about the area. Elasticsearch is helpful in combining geo-location data with full-text search, structured search, and also in doing analytics.

In this chapter, we will cover the following topics:

- Introducing geo-spatial data
- Geo-location data types
- Working with geo-point data
- Geo aggregations
- Working with geo-shapes

Introducing geo-spatial data

Geo-spatial data is information of any object on the earth and is presented by numeric values called latitude-longitude (lat-lon) that are presented on geographical systems. Apart from lat-lon, a geo-spatial object also contains other information about that object such as name, size, and shape. Elasticsearch is very helpful when working with such kinds of data. It doesn't only provide powerful geo-location searches, but also has functionalities such as sorting with geo distance, creating geo clusters, scoring based on location, and working with arbitrary geo-shapes.

Elasticsearch has two data types to solely work on geo-spatial data; they are as follows:

- **geo_point**: This is a combination of latitude-longitude pairs that defines a single location point
- **geo_shape**: This works on latitude-longitudes, but with complex shapes such as points, multi-points, lines, circles, polygons, and multi-polygons defined by a geo-JSON data structure

Working with geo-point data

Geo-points are single location points defined by a latitude-longitude pair on the surface of the earth. Using geo-points you can do the following things:

- Calculate the distance between two points
- Find the document that falls in a specified rectangular area
- Sort documents based on distance and score results based on it
- Create clusters of geo-points using aggregations

Mapping geo-point fields

Unlike all the data types in Elasticsearch, geo-point fields can't be determined dynamically. So, you have to define the mapping in advance before indexing data. The mapping for a geo-point field can be defined in the following format:

```
"location": {
    "type": "geo_point"
}
```

A geo_point mapping indexes a single field (the location in our example) in the lat-lon format. You can optionally index .lat and .lon separately by setting the lat-lon parameter to true.

Indexing geo-point data

Elasticsearch supports the following three formats to index geo_point data with the same mapping that we defined in the previous section:

```
lat-lon as a string :  "location" : "28.61, 77.23"
lat-lon as an object : "location": {
                    "lat": 28.61,
                    "lon": 77.23
                }
lat-lon as an array : "location" : [77.23, 28.61]
```

The order of latitude-longitude differs in an array format. It takes longitude first and then latitude.

Python example

In this section, we will see how to index the geo_point data in all the three formats using Python:

- Using string format:

```
doc ={"location": "28.61, 77.23"}
es.index(index=index_name, doc_type=doc_type, body=doc)
```

- Using object format:

```
location = dict()
location['lat'] = 28.61
location['lon'] = 77.23
doc['location'] = location
es.index(index=index_name, doc_type=doc_type, body=doc)
```

- Using array format:

```
location = list()
location.append(77.23)
location.append(28.6)
doc['location'] = location
es.index(index=index_name, doc_type=doc_type, body=doc)
```

Java example

- Using string format:

```
Map<String, Object> document1= new HashMap<String, Object>();
    document1.put("location", "29.9560, 78.1700");
    document1.put("name", "delhi");
    document1.put("dish_name", "chinese");
client.prepareIndex().setIndex(indexName).setType(docType)
        .setSource(document1).execute().actionGet();
```

- Using object format:

```
Map<String, Object> document3 = new HashMap<String, Object>();
Map<String, Object> locationMap = new HashMap<String, Object>();
    locationMap.put("lat", 29.9560);
    locationMap.put("lon", 78.1700);
    document3.put("location", locationMap);
    document3.put("name", "delhi");
    document3.put("dish_name", "chinese");
client.prepareIndex().setIndex(indexName).setType(docType)
        .setSource(document3).execute().actionGet();
```

- Using array format:

```
Map<String, Object> document2= new HashMap<String, Object>();
List<Double> geoPoints = new ArrayList<Double>();
    geoPoints.add(77.42);
    geoPoints.add(28.67);
  document2.put("location", geoPoints);
  document2.put("name", "delhi");
  document2.put("dish_name", "chinese");
client.prepareIndex().setIndex(indexName).setType(docType)
       .setSource(document2).execute().actionGet();
```

Querying geo-point data

The following are the query types available to query data with the `geo_point` field type:

- Geo distance query
- Geo distance range query
- Geo bounding box query

Geo distance query

The geo distance query is used to filter documents that exist within a specified distance from a given field. Let's see an example of how can we find out the best places to visit within a 200 km distance from Delhi.

Python example

```
query = {
  "query": {
    "bool": {
      "must": {
        "match_all": {}
      },
      "filter": {
        "geo_distance": {
          "distance": "200km",
          "location": {
            "lat": 28.67,
            "lon": 77.42
          }
        }
      }
    }
```

```
        }
      }
    }
response = es.search(index=index_name, doc_type=doc_type, body=query)
```

In the preceding query, we have used locations `lat-lon` in the object form; however, you always have an option to use string or array formats in the query without worrying about the format in which your data has been indexed.

The distance can be specified in various time-unit formats, such as the following:

- mi or miles for mile
- yd or yards for yard
- ft or feet for feet
- in or inch for inch
- km or kilometers for kilometer
- m or meters for meter
- cm or centimeters for centimeter
- mm or millimeters for millimeter
- NM, nmi or nauticalmiles for nautical mile

Java example

Apart from importing `QueryBuilders`, you need to have the following import in you code:

```
import org.elasticsearch.common.unit.DistanceUnit;
```

`DistanceUnit` is an Enum type that provides all the distance units that can be used.

Build the search query as follows:

```
QueryBuilder query = QueryBuilders.matchAllQuery();
```

Now, the geo distance query can be built like this:

```
QueryBuilder geoDistanceQuery =
        QueryBuilders.geoDistanceQuery("location")
        .lat(28.67).lon(77.42)
        .distance(12, DistanceUnit.KILOMETERS);
```

Combine both the queries to make a final query. Note that our geo distance query is part of a `boolQuery` that comes under the `must` block:

```
QueryBuilder finalQuery = QueryBuilders.boolQuery()
        .must(query).filter(geoDistanceQuery);
```

Here is the final execution:

```
SearchResponse response =
        client.prepareSearch(indexName).setTypes(docType)
        .setQuery(finalQuery)
        .execute().actionGet();
```

Geo distance range query

In *Chapter 3*, Putting *Elasticsearch into Action* we saw range and date range queries. The geo distance range query has the same concept. It is used to filter out documents that fall in a specified range with respect to a given point of location. For example, with the following query, you can find out the documents that fall in the range of 2,000 to 400 km from Delhi:

```
{
  "query": {
    "bool": {
      "must": {
        "match_all": {}
      },
      "filter": {
        "geo_distance_range": {
          "from": "200km",
          "to": "400km",
          "location": [77.42,28.67]
        }
      }
    }
  }
}
```

All the distance units that we have seen for the geo_distance query can be applied to this query too. This query also supports the common parameters for a range (lt, lte, gt, gte, from, to, include_upper, and include_lower).

Java example

The following example is an implementation of the same JSON query that we have seen for Python:

```
QueryBuilder query = QueryBuilders.matchAllQuery();
QueryBuilder geoDistanceRangeQuery =
        QueryBuilders.geoDistanceRangeQuery("location")
        .lon(28.67).lat(77.42)
        .from("100km").to("4000km");
QueryBuilder finalQuery = QueryBuilders.boolQuery()
```

```
        .must(query).filter(geoDistanceRangeQuery);

SearchResponse response =
        client.prepareSearch(indexName).setTypes(docType)
        .setQuery(finalQuery).execute().actionGet();
```

Geo bounding box query

This query works based on the points of a rectangle also called as bounding box. You provide the top, bottom, left, and right coordinates of the rectangle and the query compares the latitude with the left and right coordinates and the longitude with the top and bottom coordinates:

```
{
    "query": {
        "bool": {
            "must": {
                "match_all": {}
            },
            "filter": {
                "geo_bounding_box": {
                    "location": {
                        "top_left": {
                            "lat":76.9771,
                            "lon": 28.7965
                        },
                        "bottom_right": {
                            "lat": 28.4301,
                            "lon": 77.5717
                        }
                    }
                }
            }
        }
    }
}
```

See the special parameters, top_left and bottom_right, that are points of a rectangle.

These keys can also be used in an array format:

```
"top_left" : [28.7965,76.9771],
"bottom_right" : [77.5717, 28.4301]
```

They can be used in a string format as well:

```
"top_left" : "76.9771, 28.7965",
"bottom_right" : "28.4301, 77.5717"
```

Understanding bounding boxes

Initially it could be a little hard to understand and create the bounding boxes but this section will guide you in understanding and creating bounding boxes to enable you to use them in queries.

Please visit http://www.openstreetmap.org/ and on the top–left corner, click the **Export** button.

Now you can either search for a place or can manually select an area (Delhi and related areas in our example) using the corners, as shown in the following image:

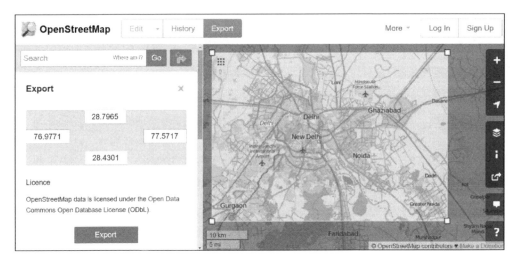

In the preceding image, you can see four points that depict the corners of the rectangle that we have drawn. The top_left point in the preceding image is 76.9771, 28.7965, whereas the **bottom_right** point is 28.4301, 77.5717.

Java example

You need to import the following additional classes in your code first:

```
import org.elasticsearch.common.geo.GeoPoint;
```

Note that Geopoint is a class in Elasticsearch that is used to create geo-points. If you do not choose to use it, you always have the lat() and lon() methods available to set the latitude and longitude points in the queries, as we have seen in the previous examples. However, for your knowledge, this example uses the GeoPoint class:

```
GeoPoint topLeft= new GeoPoint(68.91,35.60);
GeoPoint bottomRight= new GeoPoint(7.80,97.29);

QueryBuilder query = QueryBuilders.matchAllQuery();
QueryBuilder geoDistanceRangeQuery =
        QueryBuilders.geoBoundingBoxQuery("location")
        .topLeft(topLeft).bottomRight(bottomRight);
QueryBuilder finalQuery = QueryBuilders.boolQuery()
        .must(query).filter(geoDistanceRangeQuery);
SearchResponse response =
        client.prepareSearch(indexName).setTypes(docType)
        .setQuery(finalQuery)
        .execute().actionGet();
```

Sorting by distance

In the previous chapters, we saw how default sorting works on _score calculated by Elasticsearch, and we also saw how we can use the values of a field to influence the sorting of documents. Elasticsearch allows the sorting of documents by distance using the _geo_distance parameter.

For example, you want to find all the restaurants in a sorted order with respect to your current location and those that have Chinese cuisine in a list of restaurants available in your index.

Python example

```
query = {
    "query": {
      "term": {
        "dish_name": {
          "value": "chinese"
        }
      }
    },
    "sort": [
      {
        "_geo_distance": {
          "location": [
            28.67,
            77
          ],
          "order": "asc",
          "unit": "km"
        }
```

```
        }
    ]
}
response = es.search(index=index_name, doc_type=doc_type, body=query)
```

Java example

The same preceding query can be written in Java in the following way; however, first you need to import some extra classes:

```
import org.elasticsearch.search.sort.SortBuilder;
import org.elasticsearch.search.sort.SortBuilders;
import org.elasticsearch.search.sort.SortOrder;
import org.elasticsearch.common.unit.DistanceUnit;
```

We have already covered the explanation of `DistanceUnit`. `SortOrder` is also an Enum that provides different values such as `ASC` and `DESC` that can be used for sorting purposes.

Our other import, `SortBuilder`, is not only used for gro sorting, but can be also used to do sorting on other types of fields:

```
QueryBuilder query = QueryBuilders.termQuery("dish_name", "chinese");
SortBuilder sortingQuery =    SortBuilders.geoDistanceSort("location")
        .point(28.67, 77).unit(DistanceUnit.KILOMETERS)
        .order(SortOrder.ASC);
SearchResponse response =
        client.prepareSearch(indexName).setTypes(docType)
        .setQuery(query)
        .addSort(sortingQuery)
        .execute().actionGet();
```

 Please note that sorting by distance is a memory- and CPU-intensive task, so if you have a lot of documents in your index, it's better to use filters such as bounding box or queries to minimize the search context.

Geo-aggregations

Sometimes searches may return too many results but you might be just interested in finding out how many documents exist in a particular range of a location. A simple example can be to see how many news events related to crime occurred in an area by plotting them on a map or by generating a heatmap cluster of the events on the map, as shown in the following image:

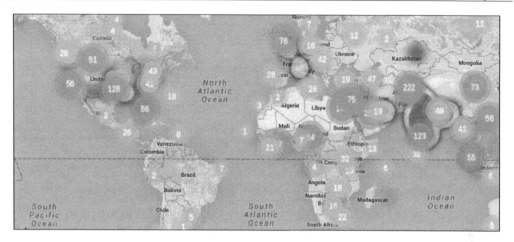

Elasticsearch offers both metric and bucket aggregations for geo_point fields.

Geo distance aggregation

Geo distance aggregation is an extension of range aggregation. It allows you to create buckets of documents based on specified ranges. Let's see how this can be done using an example.

Python example

```python
query = {
  "aggs": {
    "news_hotspots": {
      "geo_distance": {
        "field": "location",
        "origin": "28.61, 77.23",
      "unit": "km",
      "distance_type": "plane",
        "ranges": [
          {
            "to": 50
          },
          {
            "from": 50, "to": 200
          },
          {
            "from": 200
          }
        ]
      }
```

```
        }
      }
    }
```

Executing the query, as follows:

```
response = es.search(index=index_name, doc_type=doc_type, body=query,
search_type='count')
```

The preceding query creates buckets of documents with the following ranges with respect to the specified origin point:

- The count of the news events that happened in 0 to 50 km of range
- The count of the news events that happened in 50 to 200 km of range
- The count of the news events that happened outside the 200 km range

The query parameters are as follows:

- **origin**: This accepts lat-lon in all three formats: object, string or array.
- **unit**: This defaults to m (meters), but accepts other distance units as well, such as km.
- **distance_type**: This is used to specify how the distance needs to be calculated. It is an optional parameter, which defaults to `sloppy_arc` (faster but less accurate), but can also be set to `arc` (slower but most accurate) or `plane` (fastest but least accurate). Because of high error margins, plane should be used only for small geographic areas.

Java example

We covered aggregation in detail in the previous chapter, where you saw range aggregation. Geo distance aggregation is similar to it and only takes the following extra parameters:

Point, distance unit, and distance type, which we have already covered in the previous section.

For the distance type, `import org.elasticsearch.common.geo.GeoDistance;`.

```
AggregationBuilder aggregation =
  AggregationBuilders.geoDistance("news_hotspots").field(fieldName).
point(new GeoPoint(28.61, 77.23))
        .unit(DistanceUnit.KILOMETERS)
        .distanceType(GeoDistance.PLANE)
        .addUnboundedTo(50)
        .addRange(50, 100)
        .addUnboundedFrom(200);
```

```
SearchResponse response =    client.prepareSearch(indexName).
setTypes(docType)
        .setQuery(QueryBuilders.matchAllQuery())
        .addAggregation(aggregation)
        .setSize(0).execute().actionGet();
Range agg = response.getAggregations().get("news_hotspots");

for (Range.Bucket entry : agg.getBuckets()) {
    String key = entry.getKeyAsString();
    Number from = (Number) entry.getFrom();
    Number to = (Number) entry.getTo();
    long docCount = entry.getDocCount();        System.out.
println("key: "+key + " from: "+from+" to: "+to+" doc count:
"+docCount);
}
```

Using bounding boxes with geo distance aggregation

The following is an example of using a bounding box query to limit the scope of our searches and then performing aggregation.

Python example

```
query= {
  "query": {
    "bool": {
      "must": {
        "match_all": {}
      },
      "filter": {
        "geo_bounding_box": {
          "location": {
            "top_left": {"lat": 68.91, "lon": 35.6},
            "bottom_right": {"lat": 7.8, "lon": 97.29}
          }
        }
      }
    }
  },
  "aggs": {
    "news_hotspots": {
      "geo_distance": {
        "field": "location",
```

```
            "origin": "28.61, 77.23",
            "unit": "km",
            "distance_type": "plane",
            "ranges": [
               {"from": 0, "to": 50 },
               {"from": 50, "to": 200 }
            ]
         }
       }
     }
  }
}
response = es.search(index=index_name, doc_type=doc_type, body=query)
print 'total documents found', response['hits']['total']
for hit in response['hits']['hits']:
    print hit.get('_source')
```

The preceding query finds all the news documents within India (specified using the bounding box query) and creates buckets from 0 to 50 km and from 50 to 200 km in the national capital region of Delhi.

To build this query in Java, you can use the geo bounding box query in combination with geo distance aggregation examples.

Geo-shapes

Geo-shapes are completely different from geo-points. Until now we have worked with simple geo-location and rectangle searches. However, with geo-shapes, the sky is the limit. On a map, you can simply draw a line, polygon, or circle and ask Elasticsearch to populate the data according to the co-ordinates of your queries, as seen in the following image:

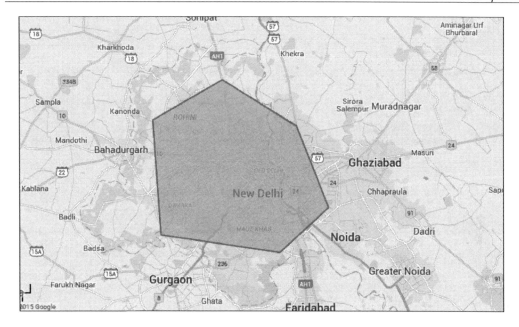

Let's see some of the most important geo-shapes.

Point

A point is a single geographical coordinate, such as your current location shown by your smart-phone. A point in Elasticsearch is represented as follows:

```
{
    "location" : {
        "type" : "point",
        "coordinates" : [28.498564, 77.0812823]
    }
}
```

Linestring

A linestring can be defined in two ways. If it contains two coordinates, it will be a straight line, but if it contains more than two points, it will be an arbitrary path:

```
{
    "location" : {
        "type" : "linestring",
        "coordinates" : [[-77.03653, 38.897676], [-77.009051,
38.889939]]
    }
}
```

Circles

A circle contains a coordinate as its centre point and a radius. For example:

```
{
    "location" : {
        "type" : "circle",
        "coordinates" : [-45.0, 45.0],
        "radius" : "500m"
    }
}
```

Polygons

A polygon is composed of a list of points with the condition that its first and last points are the same, to make it closed. For example:

```
{
  "location": {
    "type": "polygon",
    "coordinates": [
      [
        [-5.756836, 49.991408],
        [-7.250977, 55.124723],
        [1.845703, 51.500194],
        [-5.756836, 49.991408]
      ]
    ]
  }
}
```

Envelops

An envelope is a bounding rectangle and is created by specifying only the top-left and bottom-right points. For example:

```
{"location":
  {
    "type":"envelope",
    "coordinates":[[-45,45],[45,-45]]
  }
}
```

Mappings geo-shape fields

Similar to geo-points, geo-shapes are also not dynamically identified by
Elasticsearch, and a mapping needs to be defined before putting in the data.

The mapping for a geo-point field can be defined in the following format:

```
"location": {
    "type": "geo_shape",
    "tree": " quadtree "
}
```

The `tree` parameter defines which kind of grid encoding is to be used for geo-shapes. It defaults to `geo_hash`, but can also be set to `quadtree`.

Geohash versus Quadtree

Geohashes transform a two-dimension spatial point (latitude-longitude)
into an alphanumerical string or hash and is used by Elasticsearch as a
default encoding scheme for geo-point data. Geohashes divide the world
into a grid of 32 cells, and each cell is given an alphanumeric character.

Quadtrees are similar to geohashes, except that they are built on a
quadrant that is, there are only four cells at each level instead of 32. As
per my experience with geo data, quadtrees are faster and provide more
performance in comparison to geohashes.

Indexing geo-shape data

Indexing a geo-shape value in a point form is easier and follows this syntax:

```
location": {
  "type": "Point",
   "coordinates": [13.400544, 52.530286]
    }
```

Python example

The same previous location data can be used for indexing with Python in the
following way:

```
doc = dict()
location = dict()
location['coordinates'] = [13.400544, 52.530286]
doc['location'] = location
doc['location']['type'] = 'Point'
es.index(index=index_name, doc_type=doc_type, body=doc)
```

Java example

```
List<Double> coordinates = new ArrayList<Double>();
coordinates.add(13.400544);
coordinates.add(52.530286);
Map<String, Object> location = new HashMap<String, Object>();
location.put("coordinates", coordinates);
location.put("type", "Point");
Map<String, Object> document = new HashMap<String, Object>();
document.put("location", location);
IndexResponse response = client.prepareIndex().setIndex(indexName).
setType(docType)
    .setSource(document).setId("1").execute().actionGet();
```

Querying geo-shape data

Java programmers need to add the following dependencies in the pom.
xml file to be able to work with geo-spatial data. If you are using Jar
files in your class path, the Spatial4J and JTS Jar files can be found
under Elasticsearch home's lib directory:

```
<dependency>
    <groupId>com.spatial4j</groupId>
    <artifactId>spatial4j</artifactId>
    <version>0.4.1</version>
</dependency>
<dependency>
    <groupId>com.vividsolutions</groupId>
    <artifactId>jts</artifactId>
    <version>1.13</version>
    <exclusions>
        <exclusion>
            <groupId>xerces</groupId>
            <artifactId>xercesImpl</artifactId>
        </exclusion>
    </exclusions></dependency>
```

The data we have stored previously can be queried using any geo shape type.
Let's see a few examples to search the previous document in both Python and Java
languages.

Python example

Searching on `linestring` is done as follows:

```python
query = {
    "query": {
      "bool": {
        "must": {
          "match_all": {}
        },
        "filter": {
          "geo_shape": {
            "location": {
              "shape": {
                "type": "linestring",
                "coordinates": [[ 13.400544,52.530286],[13.4006,52.
5303]]
              }
            }
          }
        }
      }
    }
}
response = es.search(index=index_name, doc_type=doc_type, body=query)
```

Searching inside an envelope is done like this:

```python
query = {
    "query": {
      "bool": {
        "must": {
          "match_all": {}
        },
        "filter": {
          "geo_shape": {
            "location": {
              "shape": {
                "type": "envelope",
                "coordinates": [[13,53],[14,52]]
              }
            }
          }
        }
      }
    }
}
```

```
        }
    }
        response = es.search(index=index_name, doc_type=doc_type,
    body=query)
```

Similarly, you can search all type of shapes by specifying the type and the corresponding coordinates for that shape.

Java example

To search using `linestring`:

Apart from `QueryBuilder`, you also need to import the following statement that is used to build various geo shape queries:

```
    import org.elasticsearch.common.geo.builders.ShapeBuilder;
```

Then you can build the query, as follows:

```
QueryBuilder lineStringQuery =
    QueryBuilders.boolQuery()
    .must(QueryBuilders.matchAllQuery())
    .filter(QueryBuilders.geoShapeQuery(geoShapeFieldName,
            ShapeBuilder.newLineString()
            .point(13.400544, 52.530286)
            .point(13.4006,   52.5303)));
SearchResponse response =
        client.prepareSearch(indexName)
        .setTypes(docType)
        .setQuery(lineStringQuery)
        .execute().actionGet();
```

To search using `Envelope`:

```
QueryBuilder envelopQuery =
    QueryBuilders.boolQuery()
    .must(QueryBuilders.matchAllQuery())
    .filter(QueryBuilders.geoShapeQuery(geoShapeFieldName,
            ShapeBuilder.newEnvelope()
            .topLeft(13.0, 53.0)
            .bottomRight(14.0, 52.0)));
```

As shown in the preceding code, an envelope takes top-left and bottom-right points similar to what we saw for bounding box queries:

```
SearchResponse response =
        client.prepareSearch(indexName).setTypes(docType)
        .setQuery(envelopQuery)
        .execute().actionGet();
```

Summary

In this chapter, we learned about geo data concepts and covered the rich geo search functionalities offered by Elasticsearch, including creating mappings for geo-points and geo-shapes, indexing documents, geo-aggregations, and sorting data based on geo-distance. We also covered code examples for the most widely used geo-queries in both Python and Java.

In the next chapter, you will learn how document relationships can be managed in Elasticsearch using nested and parent-child relationships.

6
Document Relationships in NoSQL World

We have all grown up learning about relational data and databases. However, relational databases have their limitations, especially when providing full-text searches. Because of the limitations faced with relational databases, the world is adapting quickly to NoSQL solutions, and despite of there being so many NoSQL databases in the market, Elasticsearch has an upper hand because it offers the handling of relationships among different entities in combination with a powerful full-text search.

In this chapter, we will cover the following topics:

- Managing relational data in Elasticsearch
- Working with nested objects
- Introducing parent-child relationships
- Considerations for using document relationships

Relational data in the document-oriented NoSQL world

Relational databases have a lot of problems when it comes to dealing with a massive amount of data. Be it speed, efficient processing, effective parallelization, scalability, or costs, relational databases fail when the volume of data starts growing. The other challenge of relational databases is that relationships and schemas must be defined upfront. To overcome these problems, people started with normalizing data, dropping constraints, and relaxing transactional guarantees. Eventually, by compromising on these features, relational databases started resembling a NoSQL product. NoSQL is a combination of two terms, No and SQL. Some people say that it means no relational or no RDBMS, whereas other people say that it is "not only SQL". Whatever the meaning is, one thing is for sure, NoSQL is all about not following the rules of relational databases.

There is no doubt that document-oriented NoSQL databases have succeeded a lot in overcoming the issues faced in relational databases, but one thing cannot be missed out while working with any kind of data: **relationships**.

Managing relational data in Elasticsearch

Elasticsearch is also a NoSQL document data store. However, despite being a NoSQL data store, Elasticsearch offers a lot of help in managing relational data to an extent. It does support SQL-like joins and works awesomely on nested and related data entities.

For blog posts and comments, or an employee and their experiences, the data is always relational. With Elasticsearch, you can work very easily by preserving the association with different entities along with a powerful full-text search and analytics. Elasticsearch makes this possible by introducing two types of document relation models:

- Nested relationships
- Parent-child relationships

Both types of relationship work on the same model, **one to many relationship**. There is one root/parent object that can have one or more child objects.

The following image is a visual representation of how nested and parent-child documents look into Elasticsearch:

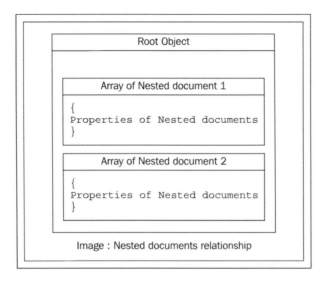

Image : Nested documents relationship

As shown in the preceding image, in a nested relationship, there is a one root object, which is the main document that we have, and it contains an array of sub-documents called nested documents. There is no limit to the level of nesting of documents inside a root object. For example, look at the following JSON for a multilevel nesting:

```
{
    "location_id": "axdbyu",
    "location_name": "gurgaon",
    "company": [
        {
            "name": "honda",
            "modelName": [
                { "name": "honda cr-v", "price": "2 million" }
            ]
        },
        {
            "name": "bmw",
            "modelName": [
                { "name": "BMW 3 Series", "price": "2 million"},
                { "name": "BMW 1 Series", "price": "3 million" }
            ]
        }
    ]
}
```

The preceding example shows that we are dealing with data in which each location can have multiple companies and each company has different models. So, indexing this kind of data without a nested type will not solve our purpose if we have to find a particular model with the name or price of a particular company at a given location. This type of relational data with a one to many relationship can be handled in Elasticsearch using nested types.

Nested fields are used to index arrays of objects, in which each object can be queried (with the nested query) as an independent document; however, in a nested structure, everything is stored in the same Lucene block. This has the advantage of fast joins while querying, but also a disadvantage of the storage of the data.

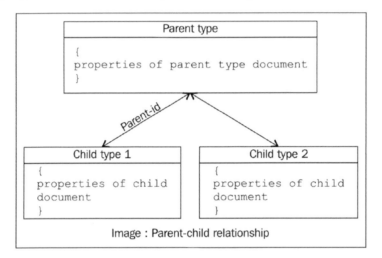

Image : Parent-child relationship

The parent-child relational model overcomes the storage problems of a nested model as the related documents here are not stored in the same lucene block, rather they are stored in the same shard. The parent and child are completely different documents. Elasticsearch maintains an internal data structure by mapping child document IDs to parent document IDs (similar to a foreign key that we use to define in relational databases).

Working with nested objects

Nested objects look similar to plain objects but they differ in mapping and the way they are stored internally in Elasticsearch.

We will work with the same Twitter data but this time we will index it in a nested structure. We will have a user as our root object and every user can have multiple tweets as nested documents. Indexing this kind of data without using nested mapping will lead to problems, as shown in the following example:

```
PUT /twitter/tweet/1
{
  "user": {
    "screen_name": "d_bharvi",
    "followers_count": "2000",
    "created_at": "2012-06-05"
  },
  "tweets": [
    {
      "id": "121223221",
      "text": "understanding nested relationships",
      "created_at": "2015-09-05"
    },
    {
      "id": "121223222",
      "text": "NoSQL databases are awesome",
      "created_at": "2015-06-05"
    }
  ]
}

PUT /twitter/tweet/2
{
  "user": {
    "screen_name": "d_bharvi",
    "followers_count": "2000",
    "created_at": "2012-06-05"
  },
  "tweets": [
    {
      "id": "121223223",
      "text": "understanding nested relationships",
      "created_at": "2015-09-05"
    },
```

```
        {
          "id": "121223224",
          "text": "NoSQL databases are awesome",
          "created_at": "2015-09-05"
        }
    ]
}
```

Now, if we want to query all the tweets that are about NoSQL and have been created on 2015-09-05, we would use the following code:

```
GET twitter/tweets/_search
{
  "query": {
    "bool": {
      "must": [
        {
          "match": {
            "tweets.text": "NoSQL"
          }
        },
        {
          "term": {
            "tweets.created_at": "2015-09-05"
          }
        }
      ]
    }
  }
}
```

The preceding query will return both the documents in the response. The reason is that Elasticsearch internally stores objects in the following way:

```
{tweets.id : ["121223221","121223222","121223223","121223224"],
tweets.text : ["understanding nested relationships",........],
tweets.created_at : ["2015-09-05","2015-06-05","2015-09-05","2015-09-
05"]}
```

All the fields of the tweet objects are flattened into an array format, which leads to loosing the association between the tweet texts and tweet creation dates, and because of this, the previous query returned the wrong results.

Creating nested mappings

The mapping for nested objects can be defined in the following way:

```
PUT twitter_nested/users/_mapping
{
  "properties": {
    "user": {
      "type": "object",
      "properties": {
        "screen_name": {
          "type": "string"
        },
        "followers_count": {
          "type": "integer"
        },
        "created_at": {
          "type": "date"
        }
      }
    },
    "tweets": {
      "type": "nested",
      "properties": {
        "id": {
          "type": "string"
        },
        "text": {
          "type": "string"
        },
        "created_at": {
          "type": "date"
        }
      }
    }
  }
}
```

In the previous mapping, user is a simple object field but the tweets field is defined as a nested type object, which contains id, text, and created_at as its properties.

Indexing nested data

You can use the same JSON documents that we used in the previous section to index users and their tweets, as indexing nested fields is similar to indexing object fields and does not require any extra effort in the code. However, Elasticsearch considers all the nested documents as separate documents and stores them internally in the following format, which preserves the relationships between tweet texts and dates:

```
{tweets.id : "121223221",tweets.text : "understanding nested
relationships", tweets.created_at : "2015-09-05"}
{tweets.id : "121223221",tweets.text : "understanding nested
relationships", tweets.created_at : "2015-09-05"}
{tweets.id : "121223221",tweets.text : "understanding nested
relationships", tweets.date : "2015-09-05"}
```

Querying nested type data

To query a nested field, Elasticsearch offers a `nested` query, which has the following syntax:

```
"query": {
    "nested": {
      "path": "path_to_nested_doc",
      "query": {}
    }
  }
```

Let's understand the `nested` query syntax:

- The top most `query` parameter wraps all the queries inside it.
- The `nested` parameter tells Elasticsearch that this query is of the nested type
- The `path` parameter specifies the path of the nested field
- The internal `query` object contains all the queries supported by Elasticsearch

Now let's run the nested query to search all the tweets that are about NoSQL and have been created on `2015-09-05`.

Python example

```
query = {
  "query": {
    "nested": {
      "path": "tweets",
      "query": {
```

```
      "bool": {
        "must": [
          {
            "match": {
              "tweets.text": "NoSQL"
            }
          },
          {
            "term": {
              "tweets.created_at": "2015-09-05"
            }
          }
        ]
      }
    }
  }
}
}
res = es.search(index='twitter_nested', doc_type= 'users', body=query)
```

Java example

```
SearchResponse response = client.prepareSearch("twitter_nested")
  .setTypes("users")
  .setQuery(QueryBuilders
  .nestedQuery(nestedField, QueryBuilders
  .boolQuery()
    .must(QueryBuilders
      .matchQuery("tweets.text", "Nosql Databases"))
    .must(QueryBuilders
      .termQuery("tweets.created_at", "2015-09-05"))))
      .execute().actionGet();
```

The response object contains the output returned from Elasticsearch, which will have one matching document in the response this time.

Nested aggregations

Nested aggregations allow you to perform aggregations on nested fields. There are two types of nested aggregations available in Elasticsearch. The first one (nested aggregation) allows you to aggregate the nested fields, whereas the second one (reverse nested aggregation) allows you to aggregate the fields that fall outside the nested scope.

Nested aggregation

A `nested` aggregation allows you to perform all the aggregations on the fields inside a `nested` object. The syntax is as follows:

```
{
  "aggs": {
    "NAME": {
      "nested": {
        "path": "path_to_nested_field"
      },
      "aggs": {}
    }
  }
}
```

Understanding nested aggregation syntax:

The syntax of a `nested` aggregation is similar to the other aggregations but here we need to specify the path of the topmost `nested` field as we have learnt to do in the `nested` queries. Once the path is specified, you can perform any aggregation on the nested documents using the inner `aggs` object. Let's see an example of how to do it:

Python example

```python
query = {
  "aggs": {
    "NESTED_DOCS": {
      "nested": {
        "path": "tweets"
      },"aggs": {
        "TWEET_TIMELINE": {
          "date_histogram": {
            "field": "tweets.created_at",
            "interval": "day"
          }
        }
      }
    }
  }
}
res = es.search(index='twitter_nested', doc_type= 'users', body=query,
size=0)
```

The preceding aggregation query creates a bucket of nested aggregation, which further contains the date histogram of tweets (the number of tweets created per day). Please note that we can combine nested aggregation with full-text search queries in a similar way to how we saw in *Chapter 4, Aggregations for Analytics.*

Java example

The following example requires this extra import in your code:

```
org.elasticsearch.search.aggregations.bucket.histogram.
DateHistogramInterval
```

You can build the aggregation in the following way:

```
SearchResponse response = client.prepareSearch("twitter_nested")
.setTypes("users")
.addAggregation(AggregationBuilders.nested("NESTED_DOCS")
.path(nestedField)
.subAggregation(AggregationBuilders
.dateHistogram("TWEET_TIMELINE")
.field("tweets.created_at")
.interval(DateHistogramInterval.DAY)
)).setSize(0).execute().actionGet();
```

 The DateHistogramInterval class offers the final static variables (DAY in our example) to define the intervals of buckets. The possible values are SECOND, MINUTE, HOUR, DAY, WEEK, MONTH, QUARTER, and YEAR.

The output for the preceding query will look like the following:

```
"aggregations" : {
    "NESTED_DOCS" : {
      "doc_count" : 2,
      "TWEET_TIMELINE" : {
        "buckets" : [ {
          "key_as_string" : "2015-09-05T00:00:00.000Z",
          "key" : 1441411200000,
          "doc_count" : 2
        } ]
      }
    }
  }
}
```

In the output, NESTED_DOCS is the name of our nested aggregations that shows doc_count as 2 because our document was composed using an array of two nested tweet documents. The TWEET_TIMELINE buckets show two documents because we have two tweets in one document.

Reverse nested aggregation

Nested aggregation has the limitation that it can only access the fields within the nested scope. Reverse nested aggregations overcome this scenario and allow you to look beyond the nested scope and go back to the root document or other nested documents.

For example, we can find all the unique users who have tweeted in a particular date range with the following reverse nested aggregation:

Python example

```python
query = {
  "aggs": {
    "NESTED_DOCS": {
      "nested": {
        "path": "tweets"
      },
      "aggs": {
        "TWEET_TIMELINE": {
          "date_histogram": {
            "field": "tweets.created_at",
            "interval": "day"
          },
          "aggs": {
            "USERS": {
              "reverse_nested": {},
              "aggs": {
                "UNIQUE_USERS": {
                  "cardinality": {
                    "field": "user.screen_name"
                  }
                }
              }
            }
          }
        }
      }
    }
  }
}
resp = es.search(index='twitter_nested', doc_type= 'users',
body=query, size=0)
```

Java example

```
SearchResponse response =
        client.prepareSearch(indexName).setTypes(docType)
    .addAggregation(AggregationBuilders.nested("NESTED_DOCS")
    .path(nestedField)
    .subAggregation(AggregationBuilders.dateHistogram("TWEET_TIMELINE")
.field("tweets.created_at").interval(DateHistogramInterval.DAY)
    .subAggregation(AggregationBuilders.reverseNested("USERS")
    .subAggregation(AggregationBuilders.cardinality("UNIQUE_USERS")
.field("user.screen_name")))))
    .setSize(0).execute().actionGet();
```

The output for the preceding aggregation will be as follows:

```
{   "aggregations": {
      "NESTED_DOCS": {
        "doc_count": 2,
        "TWEET_TIMELINE": {
          "buckets": [
            {
              "key_as_string": "2015-09-05T00:00:00.000Z",
              "key": 1441411200000,
              "doc_count": 2,
              "USERS": {
                "doc_count": 1,
                "UNIQUE_USERS": {
                  "value": 1
      }
    }
  }             ]        }    }  }  }
```

The preceding output shows the nested docs count as 2, whereas the USERS key specifies that there is only one root document that exists in the given time range. UNIQUE_USERS shows the cardinality aggregation output for the unique users in the index.

Parent-child relationships

Similar to nested types, parent-child relationships also allow you to relate different entities together but they differ in the implementation and behavior. Unlike nested documents, they are not present within the same document, rather parent-child documents are completely separate documents. They follow the one to many relationship principle and allow you to define one type as parent and one or more as the child type.

Creating parent-child mappings

To create a parent-child mapping, you just need to specify which type should be the parent of the child type. You do not need to define anything extra in the parent type mapping but before indexing the data in the child type, you need to specify in the child's mapping who will be its parent.

Let's create a new index, `twitter_parent_child`:

```
PUT /twitter_parent_child
```

Now, put the mapping of the tweets type by specifying that the `user` will be its parent. This is done using the `_parent` keyword inside the mapping, but outside the properties:

```
PUT /twitter_parent_child/tweets/_mapping
{
  "_parent": {
    "type": "users"
  },
  "properties": {
    "text":{"type": "string"},
    "created_at":{"type": "date"}
  }
}
```

Next, put the mapping of the users type:

```
PUT /twitter_parent_child/users/_mapping
{
  "properties": {
    "screen_name":{"type": "string"},
    "created_at":{"type": "date"}
  }
}
```

> One parent can have multiple child types but one child can have only one parent type. It's also important to know the fact that you have to create the mappings for child type and specify the parent before creating the parent type. If you do it in reverse, you will get the exception: "Can't add a `_parent` field that points to an already existing type". Also, note that parents cannot be updated for any child type.

Indexing parent-child documents

Indexing parent documents is similar to what we have followed till now. However, while indexing children, you need to specify the unique ID of the parent document so that Elasticsearch can know which document is the parent of this document.

Python example

Indexing parent document:

A parent document is indexed in a similar way to any other document:

```
parent_doc = {}
parent_doc['screen_name'] = 'd_bharvi'
parent_doc['followers_count"'] = 2000
parent_doc['create_at"'] = '2012-05-30'
es.index(index='twitter_parent_child', doc_type= users, body=parent_
doc, id='64995604')
```

Indexing a child document:

Indexing a child document requires specifying the _id of the parent document type. In Python, it is done using the id parameter inside the index function:

```
child_doc = {}
child_doc['text'] = 'learning parent-child concepts'
child_doc['created_at'] = '2015-10-30'
es.index(index='twitter_parent_child', doc_type= 'tweets', body=child_
doc, id = '2333', parent='64995604')
```

Java example

Include the following import statements:

```
import org.elasticsearch.action.index.IndexRequestBuilder;
```

The parent document can be indexed in the following way:

```
IndexRequestBuilder index = client.prepareIndex(
"twitter_parent_child", "users");
Map<String, Object> parentDoc= new HashMap<String, Object>();
parentDoc.put("screen_name", "d_bharvi");
parentDoc.put("followers_count", 2000);
parentDoc.put("create_at", "2012-05-30");
index.setId("64995604").setSource(parentDoc)
.execute().actionGet();
```

The child document can be indexed in the following way:

```
IndexRequestBuilder index=client.prepareIndex("twitter_parent_child",
"tweets");
Map<String, Object> childDoc= new HashMap<String, Object>();
childDoc.put("text", "learning parent-child concepts in
elasticsearch");
childDoc.put("create_at", "2015-05-30");
index.setParent("64995604").setId("2333")
.setSource(childDoc).execute().actionGet();
```

Please note that while indexing the child document, we have used the `setParent` method and passed the `_id` of the parent document.

 By specifying the parent ID, we not only create an association between the parent and child documents but also make sure that they reside in the same shard.

Querying parent-child documents

Elasticsearch offers two queries to search parent-child documents:

- The `has_child` query
- The `has_parent` query

has_child query

The `has_child` query allows you to find and return parent documents by querying the child type. For example, we can find all the users who have tweeted about Elasticsearch.

Python example

```
query = {
  "query": {
    "has_child": {
      "type": "tweets",
      "query": {
        "match": {
          "text": "elasticsearch"
        }
      }
    }
  }
}
```

```
        }
    }
resp = es.search(index='twitter_parent_child', doc_type= 'users',
body=query)
```

Java example

The same query can be applied using Java with the following code:

```
SearchResponse response = client.prepareSearch("twitter_parent_
child").setTypes("users")
    .setQuery(QueryBuilders.hasChildQuery(childType,    QueryBuilders.mat
chQuery("text","elasticsearch")))
    .execute().actionGet();
```

 Please see carefully that while using the has_child query, it is applied to the parent type because we have to return the parent documents, while the has_child parameter contains the name of the child type.

has_parent query

The has_parent query works in reverse compared to the has_child query and allows you to find and return child documents by querying on the parent type. For example, we can find all the tweets tweeted by users who have a followers count greater than 200.

Python example

```
query = {
  "query": {
    "has_parent": {
      "type": "users",
      "query": {
        "range": {
          "followers_count": {
            "gte": 200
          }
        }
      }
    }
  }
}
resp = es.search(index='twitter_parent_child', doc_type= 'tweets',
body=query)
```

Java example

The same query can be applied using Java with the following code:

```
SearchResponse response = client.prepareSearch("twitter_parent_child")
    .setTypes("tweets")
    .setQuery(QueryBuilders
    .hasParentQuery(parentType, QueryBuilders.rangeQuery("followers_
count")
    .gt(200))).execute().actionGet();
```

Considerations for using document relationships

Over the years, Elasticsearch has improved a lot in reducing memory pressure by introducing doc_values, which is a little slower than the in-memory data structure, fielddata, but still offer reasonable speed and performance. However, because of the way nested and parent-child documents are stored and searched, you should keep the pros and cons in mind before modeling your data. The following is a comparison of nested versus parent-child types, which is nicely outlined by Zachary Tong in one of his articles:

Nested	Parent-Child
Stored in the same Lucene block as each other, which helps in a faster read/query performance. Reading a nested doc is faster than the equivalent parent/child.	Children are stored separately from the parent, but are routed to the same shard. So parent/children performance is slightly less on read/query than nested.
Updating a single field in a nested document (parent or nested children) forces ES to re-index the entire nested document. This can be very expensive for large nested docs.	If you are not using doc_values (which is by default since version 2.0.0), parent/child mappings have a bit extra memory overhead since ES maintains a "join" list in the memory.
This is best suited for data that does not change frequently.	Updating a child doc does not affect the parent or any other children, which can potentially save a lot of indexing on large docs.

Summary

This chapter covered the concepts of handling relational data in Elasticsearch with the help of nested and parent-child types. We learned about creating mappings, indexing, and querying data using Java and Python. This chapter also covered the pros and cons of using these relationships in Elasticsearch.

In the next chapter, we will learn about the different types of search execution offered by Elasticsearch and write code to re-index data from one index to other.

7
Different Methods of Search and Bulk Operations

The use cases of different searches differ according to scenarios, and Elasticsearch provides a lot of flexibility regarding how a user can perform search requests and return the data for efficient processing. The other most important thing to know is the execution of bulk operations, which enables you to finish your tasks quickly and do some other important work in your life.

In this chapter, we will cover the following topics:

- Introducing search types in Elasticsearch
- Cheaper CRUD bulk operations
- Multi get and multi search APIs
- Data pagination and re-indexing
- Practical considerations for bulk processing

Introducing search types in Elasticsearch

Elasticsearch provides the following search types to be executed:

- `query_then_fetch`: This is the default search type available in Elasticsearch. It follows a two-phase search execution. In the first phase (`query`), the query goes to a coordinating node that further forwards the query to all the relevant shards. Each shard searches the documents, sorts them locally, and returns the results to the coordinating node. The coordinating node further merges all the results, sorts them, and returns the result to the caller. The final results are of the maximum size specified in the size parameter with the search request.

- `dfs_query_then_fetch`: This is similar to the `query_then_fetch` search type, but asks Elasticsearch to do some extra processing for more accurate scoring of documents. In the `fetch` phase, all the shards compute the distributed term frequencies.

- `scan`: The scan search type differs from normal search requests because it does not involve any scoring and sorting processing of the documents. `scan` is used for the scenarios where scoring is not required and you need to iterate over a large number of documents from Elasticsearch.

The deprecated search type: count

There used to be another search type, `count`, that was used to return just the count of documents for a given query. It was also used while doing aggregation for excluding documents in a result and only returning the aggregation results. `Count` has been deprecated from Elasticsearch version 2.0 and will be removed in upcoming releases. You just need to use the `size` parameter of `0` in your query instead of using the `count` search type.

Search types can be specified while executing your search with the `search_type` parameter in the following way:

- Using REST endpoint:

```
GET /search/search_type=scan
```

- Using Python client:

```
es.search(index=index_name, doc_type=doc_type, body=query, search_
type='scan'
```

- Using Java client, first import `SearchType` using the following import statement:

```
import org.elasticsearch.action.search.SearchType;
```

- Then, do the following:

```
client.prepareSearch("index_name")
.setTypes("doc_type")
.setSearchType(SearchType.SCAN)
.setQuery(QueryBuilders.matchAllQuery())
.execute().actionGet();
```

Cheaper bulk operations

There are times when you need to perform more than one request on Elasticsearch. For this, Elasticsearch offers a bulk API with the `_bulk` endpoint that allows you to perform bulk operations in a single request, be it indexing, updating, or deleting more than one document, getting more than one document using more than one document ID, or executing more than one query in a single request. The best part is that bulk operations can be executed on more than one `index` and `doc` type in a single request. The Elasticsearch Java client also offers a `BulkProcessor` class, which will be covered in a later section of this chapter. For now, let's explore the bulk requests.

 The Python client provides a helper module to create bulk operations. You need to import this module `from elasticsearch.helpers import bulk`.

Bulk create

`Bulk create` allows to create documents only if they do not already exist in the index. It expects `_source` for each document to be separated with new lines.

Python example:

1. Declare a list to hold the document set, as follows:

   ```
   docs = []
   ```

2. Create documents with the following:

   ```
   doc1 = dict()
   doc1['text'] = 'checking out search types in elasticsearch'
   doc1['created_at'] = datetime.datetime.utcnow()
   doc2 = dict()
   doc2['text'] = 'bulk API is awesome'
   doc2['created_at'] = datetime.datetime.utcnow()
   ```

3. Add both the documents to a list of documents:

   ```
   docs.append(doc1)
   docs.append(doc2)
   ```

4. Declare a list that will hold the actions to be executed in the `bulk`:

   ```
   actions = list()
   ```

5. Create an action for each document and append it to the list of `bulk` actions:

```
for doc in docs:
    action = {
    '_index': index_name,
    '_type': doc_type,
    '_op_type': 'create',
    '_source': doc
    }
    actions.append(action)
```

Please note that if you use `_op_type` as `index`, it will be of the `index` type bulk request. Now, execute the `bulk` method of the Elasticsearch helpers module to index the documents in a single request:

```
try:
    bulk_response = helpers.bulk(es, actions,request_timeout=100)
    print "bulk response:",bulk_response
except Exception as e:
    print str(e)
```

 If the bulk size is more than 500, the Python module of Elasticsearch internally breaks the bulk requests into chunks of 500 documents and then indexes them.

Java example:

1. Create an object of the `BulkRequestBuilder` class:

```
BulkRequestBuilder bulkRequests = client.prepareBulk();
```

2. Create two documents using `hashmap`, as follows:

```
Map<String, Object> document1= new HashMap<String, Object>();
Map<String, Object> document2= new HashMap<String, Object>();
document1.put("screen_name", "d_bharvi");
document1.put("followers_count", 2000);
document1.put("create_at", "2015-09-20");
document2.put("screen_name", "b44nz0r");
document2.put("followers_count", 6000);
document2.put("create_at", "2019-09-20");
```

3. Create individual index requests and add them to the bulk request:

```
bulkRequests.add(new IndexRequest().index(indexName).
type(docType).source(document1).opType("create").id("125"));

bulkRequests.add(new IndexRequest().index(indexName).
type(docType).source(document1).opType("index").id("123"));
```

4. Execute the bulk request, as shown here:

```
BulkResponse bulkResponse =bulkRequests.execute().actionGet();

if (bulkResponse.hasFailures())
  {
    //handle the failure scenarios
    for (BulkItemResponse bulkItemResponse : bulkResponse) {

    }
  }
```

Bulk indexing

Bulk indexing allows you to index multiple documents in a single request, which is similar to indexing a single document as we have seen until now. If the document already exists, it deletes the document and indexes a new document in its place, and if the document does not already exist, it creates a new document. It also expects _source for each document to be separated with new lines.

The code for bulk index is the same as for bulk create, with only one difference: in Python, you just need to set the _op_type value to index, and in Java opType will take index as its parameter. The difference between index and create is: when the operation is set to index, documents get over-ridden if they already exist in the index, whereas a create operation is useful when you want to skip the indexing of documents that already exist. Therefore, the create operation gives a performance boost in comparison to index.

Bulk updating

Bulk updating allows you to perform partial updates on one or more than one document in a single request. Instead of _source, it requires either a script parameter or a doc parameter to update the documents.

Python example:

1. Declare a list that will hold the actions to be executed in the `bulk`:

```
actions = list()
```

2. Create an action for each document and append it to the list of bulk actions:

```
for doc in docs:
    action = {
    '_index': index_name,
    '_type': doc_type,
    '_id': doc_id,
    '_op_type': 'update',
    'doc': {'new_field': 'doing partial update with a new field'}
    }
    actions.append(action)
```

As mentioned earlier, a partial update requires `doc` instead of `_source` as a new field to be updated when an ID for the existing documents is provided. The same is shown in the preceding example. For every document, we have created an inline partial `doc` with the field name as `new field`, and once the actions are created, we are all set to execute a bulk update as follows:

```
try:
    bulk_indexed = helpers.bulk(es, actions, request_timeout=100)
    print "bulk response:", bulk_indexed
except Exception as e:
    print str(e)
```

You will get a missing document exception if the document ID does not exist in the index.

Java example

In Java, you can create individual bulk requests using `UpdateRequest` and add them to the object of `BulkRequestBuilder`, using the following code:

```
bulkRequests.add(new UpdateRequest().index(indexName).type(docType).
doc(partialDoc1).id("125"));

bulkRequests.add(new UpdateRequest().index(indexName).type(docType).
doc(partialDoc2).id("123"));
```

Finally, bulk updates can be executed similarly to what we saw for bulk indexing:

```
BulkResponse bulkResponse = bulkRequests.execute().actionGet();

if (bulkResponse.hasFailures())
  {
    //handle the failure scenarios
    for (BulkItemResponse bulkItemResponse : bulkResponse) {

    }
  }
```

Bulk deleting

Bulk deleting allows you to delete one or more than one document in a single request. It does not require any source in the request body and follows the same semantic as a standard delete request.

Python example:

Bulk deleting needs the IDs of documents to be deleted, which you can do as follows:

```
del_complete_batch = []
for id in ids_to_delete:
    del_complete_batch.append({
            '_op_type': 'delete',
            '_index': index_name,
            '_type': doc_type,
            '_id': id,
        })
try:
    helpers.bulk(es, del_complete_batch, request_timeout=100)
except Exception as e:
    print str(e)
```

Java example:

Bulk delete requests can be built by creating individual DeleteRequest and adding them to the BulkRequestBuilder object:

```
bulkRequests.add(new DeleteRequest().index(indexName).type(docType).
id("1252"));

bulkRequests.add(new UpdateRequest().index(indexName).type(docType).
id("123"));
And once the bulk is ready, then can be executed.
BulkResponse bulkResponse = bulkRequests.execute().actionGet();
```

Please note that the execution might return an exception similar to bulk updates if the documents do not exist in the index.

Multi get and multi search APIs

Until now, you have seen the execution of a single get request to fetch a document and hit a single query at a time to search for documents. However, life will be easier with the following two APIs offered by Elasticsearch.

Multi get

Multi get is all about combining more than one get request in a single request. I remember once I had a requirement to check the existence of multiple documents in an index and create a bulk update request against only those IDs that did not already exist. The one way to do this was by hitting a single HEAD request for each document ID, and based on the response of Elasticsearch, create a bulk update request for the documents that did not exist. However, multi get requests can solve this problem in a single API call instead of multiple HEAD requests.

All you need to do is create an array of document IDs and hit them on Elasticsearch using the _mget endpoint of Elasticsearch. The following is a simple curl request to show how you can do this:

```
curl 'localhost:9200/index_name/doc_type/_mget' -d '{
    "ids" : ["1", "2"]
}'
```

Here, IDs are the _id of the documents to be fetched.

 If an ID does not exist in the index, Elasticsearch returns found=false for that document ID.

You have additional options to decide whether you want to return the data of the document or not. If it is not required, just set _source : false while hitting the mget request. For example:

```
curl 'localhost:9200/index_name/doc_type/_mget' -d '{
    "ids" : ["1", "2"], "_source" : false
}'
```

If you are interested in only returning a particular field, you can do it like this:

```
curl 'localhost:9200/index_name/doc_type/_mget' -d '{
    "ids" : ["1", "2"], "_source" : ["field1", "field2"]
}
```

Here, `field1` and `field2` are the names of the fields required to be returned.

Python example:

Declare an array of IDs to be fetched:

```
document_ids_to_get = ['1','4','12','54','123','543']
```

Create a query by passing an array of doc IDs to the ID parameter:

```
query = {"ids": document_ids_to_get}
#Exceute the query using mget endpoint:
exists_resp = es.mget(index=index_name,doc_type=doc_type, body=query,
_source=False, request_timeout=100)
```

Java example:

Import the following packages into your source code:

```
import org.elasticsearch.action.get.MultiGetItemResponse;
import org.elasticsearch.action.get.MultiGetResponse;
```

Create a multi get request in the following way:

```
MultiGetResponse responses = client.prepareMultiGet()
        .add(indexName, docType, ids_to_be_fetched)
        .execute().actionGet();
```

The multi get response is parsed in the following way:

```
for (MultiGetItemResponse itemResponse : responses) {
    GetResponse response = itemResponse.getResponse();
    if (response.isExists()) {
        String json = response.getSourceAsString();
        System.out.println(json);
    }
}
```

The `id_to_be_fetched` function is a list of document IDs that need to be fetched.

Multi searches

You might have worked with many databases and search engines, but none of them provides the functionality to hit more than one query in a single request. Elasticsearch can do this with its `_msearch` REST API. For this, it follows a specific request format as shown here:

```
header\n
body\n
........
........
header\n
body\n
```

Understanding the preceding search request structure:

- `header`: This includes the name of the index/indices to be searched upon and optionally includes the search type, search preference nodes (primary, secondary, and so on), and routing
- `body`: This includes the search request queries

Let's see an example:

1. Create a file, `multi_requests`, with the following content. Please note that each line is separated with \n (new line):

```
{"index" : "users"}
{"query" : {"match_all" : {}}, "from" : 0, "size" : 10}
{"index" : "twitter", "search_type" : "dfs_query_then_fetch"}
{"query" : {"match_all" : {}}}
```

2. Now execute the search request using the `_msearch` API:

```
curl -XGET localhost:9200/_msearch --data-binary "@ multi _
requests"
```

In the preceding `curl` command, we have used the `–data-binary` flag to load the multiline content from the file. This is required while executing bulk data indexing too.

Searches executed with the `_msearch` API return responses in the responses array form, which includes the search response for each search request that matches its order in the original `multi search` request. If there is a complete failure for that specific search request, an object with an error message will be returned in the place of the actual search response.

Python example:

1. Create an individual request head with an index name and doc type in the
   following way:

   ```
   req_head1 = {'index': index_name1, 'type': doc_type1}
   ```

2. Create a `query_request_array` list, which contains the actual queries and
   the head part of those queries:

   ```
   query_request_array = []
   query_1 = {"query" : {"match_all" : {}}}
   query_request_array.append(req_head1)
   query_request_array.append(query_1)
   ```

3. Create another request with a head and body:

   ```
   req_head2 = {'index': index_name2, 'type': doc_typ2}
   query_2 = {"query" : {"match_all" : {}}}
   query_request_array.append(req_head2)
   query_request_array.append(query_2)
   ```

4. Execute the request using a `msearch` endpoint by passing `query_request_`
   `array` into the body; you can optionally set `request_timeout` too:

   ```
   response = es.msearch(body=query_request_array)
   ```

5. The response of a multi search can be parsed in the following way:

   ```
   for resp in response["responses"]:
       if resp.get("hits"):
           for hit in resp.get("hits").get('hits'):
               print hit["_source"]
   ```

Java example:

1. To execute a multi search using Java, you need to import the following
   packages into your code:

   ```
   import org.elasticsearch.action.search.MultiSearchResponse;
   import org.elasticsearch.action.search.SearchRequestBuilder;
   ```

2. Then, you can create an individual search request using the
   `SearchRequestBuilder` class:

   ```
   SearchRequestBuilder searchRequest1 = client.
   prepareSearch().setIndices(indexName).setTypes(docType)
   .setQuery(QueryBuilders.queryStringQuery("elasticsearch").
   defaultField("text")).setSize(1);

   SearchRequestBuilder searchRequest2 =
   ```

```
client.prepareSearch().setIndices(indexName).setTypes(docType)
        .setQuery(QueryBuilders.matchQuery("screen_name", "d_
bharvi")).setSize(1);
```

3. These individual search requests can be added to a multi search request and executed in the following way:

```
MultiSearchResponse sr = client.prepareMultiSearch()
               .add(searchRequest1)
               .add(searchRequest1)
               .execute().actionGet();
```

4. You will get all the individual responses from `MultiSearchResponse`, as follows:

```
long nbHits = 0;
for (MultiSearchResponse.Item item : sr.getResponses()) {
    SearchResponse response = item.getResponse();
    nbHits += response.getHits().getTotalHits();
    }
 }
```

Data pagination

We have seen that for any query, Elasticsearch by default returns only the top 10 documents after scoring and sorting them. However, they are not always enough to serve the purpose. A user always needs more and more data either to render on a page or to process in the backend. Let's see how we can do this.

Pagination with scoring

In the previous chapters, we discussed how Elasticsearch offers the `from` and `to` parameters to be passed with search requests. So, you always have an option to either increase the `size` parameter to load more results from Elasticsearch or send another query with the changed `from` and `size` values to get more data.

This pagination approach makes sense when you have to fetch a limited number of documents from Elasticsearch. As this approach is too costly and can kill Elasticsearch if you are hitting a request, for example, where `from = 100000` and `size = 100010` to get 10 documents, which have less score than those `1 lac` documents in the index.

Pagination without scoring

While working with Elasticsearch, a functionality that is needed most of the time is: returning a large set of data to process or to simply re-index from one index to another. This type of data fetching does not require any document scoring or sorting. Elasticsearch offers a scan search type to fulfil this requirement.

Scrolling and re-indexing documents using scan-scroll

A scan search type works in the same manner as how you scan a Facebook or Twitter web page with your eyes and scroll to see more content.

Python example:

You can define a query for which you want all the documents to be returned, as follows:

```
query = {"query":{"match_all":{}}}
```

Also, you can create a list that will hold the returned documents:

```
documents = []
```

Then execute the following request to get the scroll ID from Elasticsearch, which will be used to get the actual data in subsequent requests. The `scroll` parameter (timeout for scrolling) in the following request specifies for how long the scroll will be open. It can be defined using `100s` (100 seconds) or `2m` (two minutes):

```
resp = es.search(index=source_index, doc_type=source_doc_type,
body=query, search_type="scan", scroll='100s', size=100)
```

Once `scroll_id` is returned with the preceding request, you can use it inside a `while` loop, which will run until Elasticsearch returns the entire document for your query:

```
while True:
    print 'scrolling for ',str(scroll_count)+' time'
  #A new scroll id generated for each request. Scroll parameter is
also need to be set for each request.
    resp = es.scroll(resp['_scroll_id'], scroll='100s')
    if len(resp['hits']['hits']) == 0:
        print 'data re-indexing completed..!!'
        break
    else:
      #add the documents to the documents list
        documents.extend(resp['hits']['hits'])
```

```
        #send the documens to for re-indexing
        perform_bulk_index(destination_index, destination_doc_type,
    documents)
        #Empty your documents list so that it can hold another batch of
    response
        documents = []
```

The `perform_bulk_index` function can be implemented in the same way as we have seen in bulk indexing. It will take a set of documents and will be sent to Elasticsearch in bulk:

```
actions = []
for document in documents:
    actions.append({
            '_op_type': 'create',
            '_index': destination_index,
            '_type': destination_doc_type,
            '_id': document['_id'],
            '_source': document['_source']
            })
try:
    helpers.bulk(es, actions, request_timeout=100)
except Exception as e:
    print "bulk index raised exception", str(e)
```

Java Example (using bulk processor):

We have already seen how bulk indexing can be done using `BulkRequestBuilder`. You will now learn how to do bulk indexing using the `BulkProcessor` class.

As mentioned in the Elasticsearch documentation:

> *"A bulk processor is a thread safe bulk processing class, allowing you to easily set when to "flush a new bulk request (either based on number of actions, based on the size, or time), and to easily control the number of concurrent bulk requests allowed to be executed in parallel."*

The most important parameters offered by `BulkProcessor` are as follows:

- **Bulk actions**: This defaults to 1,000. This sets the number of operations to be processed in a single bulk request.
- **Flush interval**: The default for this is not set. Flush is a process of performing a Lucene commit on the disk. Before doing a flush, Elasticsearch stores the data inside a special file called `translog` to prevent data loss.

- **Bulk size**: This defaults to 5 MB. This specifies how much data should be flushed at once. It should be increased wisely according to the capacity of the Elasticsearch cluster.

- **Concurrent Requests**: The default value is 1. (It should not be set to more than the number of available CPU cores where code is running because each concurrent request starts a new thread.)

Let's import the packages into our code to get data through `scan-scroll` and `bulk` processing:

```
import static org.elasticsearch.index.query.QueryBuilders.
matchAllQuery;
import java.util.concurrent.TimeUnit;
import org.elasticsearch.action.bulk.BulkProcessor;
import org.elasticsearch.action.bulk.BulkRequest;
import org.elasticsearch.action.bulk.BulkResponse;
import org.elasticsearch.action.index.IndexRequest;
import org.elasticsearch.action.search.SearchResponse;
import org.elasticsearch.action.search.SearchType;
import org.elasticsearch.client.Client;
import org.elasticsearch.common.unit.TimeValue;
import org.elasticsearch.search.SearchHit;
```

The following are the main variables you need to declare to index using a bulk processor:

```
//The maximum time to wait for the bulk requests to complete
    public static final int SCROLL_TIMEOUT_SECONDS = 30;
    //Number of documents to be returned, maximum would be scroll_
size*number of shards
    public static final int SCROLL_SIZE = 10;
    //Sets when to flush a new bulk request based on the number of
actions currently added. defaults to 1000
    public static final int BULK_ACTIONS_THRESHOLD = 10000;
    //Sets the number of concurrent requests allowed to be executed.
    public static final int BULK_CONCURRENT_REQUESTS = 2;
    //Sets a flush interval flushing (specified in seconds)
    public static final int BULK_FLUSH_DURATION = 30;
```

Create an instance of the `Bulk Processor` class using the previous variables:

```
BulkProcessor bulkProcessor = BulkProcessor.builder(clientTo,
                createLoggingBulkProcessorListener()).
setBulkActions(BULK_ACTIONS_THRESHOLD).setConcurrentRequests(BULK_
CONCURRENT_REQUESTS)
        .setFlushInterval(createFlushIntervalTime().build();
```

Getting the data from scan-scroll can be done as follows:

```
SearchResponse searchResponse = clientFrom.prepareSearch(fromIndex)
        .setTypes(sourceDocType)
            .setQuery(matchAllQuery())
            .setSearchType(SearchType.SCAN)
            .setScroll(createScrollTimeoutValue())
            .setSize(SCROLL_SIZE).execute().actionGet();
```

This will return a scroll ID, which will be used to scroll the documents and return them for processing:

```
while (true) {
        searchResponse = clientFrom.prepareSearchScroll(searchResp
onse.getScrollId())
                .setScroll(createScrollTimeoutValue()).execute().
actionGet();
        if (searchResponse.getHits().getHits().length == 0) {
            System.out.println("Closing the bulk processor");
            bulkProcessor.close();
            break; //Break condition: No hits are returned
        }
        //Add the documents to the bulk processor and depending on
the bulk threshold they will be flushed to ES
        for (SearchHit hit : searchResponse.getHits()) {
    IndexRequest request = new IndexRequest(toIndex,
destinationDocType, hit.id());
            request.source(hit.getSource());
            bulkProcessor.add(request);
            }
        }
```

The bulk processor has a listener, which flushes the request index depending on the bulk threshold. This listener can be defined in the following way:

```
private BulkProcessor.Listener createLoggingBulkProcessorListener() {
        return new BulkProcessor.Listener() {
        @Override
        public void beforeBulk(long executionId, BulkRequest request)
    {
```

```
        System.out.println("Going to execute new bulk composed "+
request.numberOfActions()+" no. of actions");
        }

    @Override
    public void afterBulk(long executionId, BulkRequest request,
BulkResponse response) {
        System.out.println("Executed bulk composed "+ request.
numberOfActions()+" no. of actions");
        }

    @Override
    public void afterBulk(long executionId, BulkRequest request,
Throwable failure) {
        System.out.println("Error executing bulk "+ failure);
        }
    };
}
```

You also need to define the following helper function to create time units to be used by bulk processing:

```
private TimeValue createFlushIntervalTime() {
    return new TimeValue(BULK_FLUSH_DURATION, TimeUnit.SECONDS);
}

private TimeValue createScrollTimeoutValue() {
    return new TimeValue(SCROLL_TIMEOUT_SECONDS, TimeUnit.
SECONDS);
}
```

Practical considerations for bulk processing

It's awesome to minimize the requests using the search types and bulk APIs we saw in this chapter, but you also need to think that for a large amount of processing to be done by Elasticsearch, you need to take care of resource utilization and control the size of your requests accordingly. The following are some points that will help you while working with the things you have learned in this chapter.

The most important factor to be taken care of is the size of your documents. Fetching or indexing 1 KB of 1,000 documents in a single request is damn easier than 100 KB of 1,000 documents:

- **Multisearch**: While querying with multi search requests, you should take care of how many queries you are hitting in a single request. You just can't combine 1,000 queries in a single query and execute them in one go. Also, the number of queries should be minimized according to the complexity of queries. So, you can break your query set into multiple multi-search requests in batches of, for example, 100 queries per batch, and execute them. You can combine the results after all the batches are executed. The same rule applies while querying with the mget API too.

- **Scan-scroll**: A search with scan and scroll is highly beneficial for performing deep paginations, but the number of documents returned in a single request is usually *scroll_size*number_of_shards*. We have also seen that we need to pass the timeout using a scroll parameter because it tells Elasticsearch for how long a search context needs to be open on the server to serve a particular scroll request. Scroll timeouts do not need to be long enough to process all the data — they just need to be long enough to process the previous batch of results. Each scroll request (with the scroll parameter) sets a new expiry time. So, you need to set the scroll timeout wisely so that there are not too many open search contexts existing at the same time on your Elasticsearch server. This heavily affects the background merge process of Lucene indexes. Also, the scroll time should not be so small that your request gets a timeout.

- **Bulk indexing and bulk updates**: Sending too much data in a single request can harm your Elasticsearch node if you do not have the optimal resources available. Remember that while data indexing or updating, the merging of Lucene segments is done in the background, and with a large amount of data merging and flushing on the disk, a very high amount of CPU and disk IO is required. So, choose the numbers wisely by benchmarking your requests.

Summary

This chapter provided you some very important functionalities of Elasticsearch, which every programmer needs to know while developing applications in real-time scenarios and working with a large number of datasets. We covered the bulk APIs by combining multiple requests into a single one to reduce the time and number of requests to process large datasets. We also saw some best practices to be kept in mind while working with these APIs, and most importantly, you got practical code examples that will help you through your journey with Elasticsearch.

In the next chapter, you are going to learn about search relevancy and how to control the scoring of your searches.

8
Controlling Relevancy

Getting a search engine to behave can be very hard. It does not matter if you are a newbie or have years of experience with Elasticsearch or Solr, you must have definitely struggled with low-quality search results in your application. The default algorithm of Lucene does not come close to meeting your requirements, and there is always a struggle to deliver the relevant search results.

In this chapter, we will cover the following topics:

- Introducing relevant searches
- Out-of-the-box tools from Elasticsearch
- Controlling relevancy with custom scoring

Introducing relevant searches

Relevancy is the root of a search engine's value proposition and can be defined as the art of ranking content for a user's search based on how much that content satisfies the needs of the user or the business.

In an application, it does not matter how beautiful your user interface looks or how many functionalities you are providing to the user; search relevancy cannot be avoided at any cost. So, despite of the mystical behavior of search engines, you have to find a solution to get relevant results. The relevancy becomes more important because a user does not care about the whole bunch of documents that you have. The user enters their keywords, selects filters, and focuses on a very small amount of data—the relevant results. And if your search engine fails to deliver according to expectations, the user might be annoyed, which might be a loss for your business.

A search engine like Elasticsearch comes with a built-in intelligence. You enter the keyword and within the blink of an eye, it returns to you the results that it thinks are relevant according to its intelligence. However, Elasticsearch does not have a built-in intelligence according to your application domain. The relevancy is not defined by a search engine; rather it is defined by your users, their business needs, and the domains. Take an example of Google or Twitter; they have put in years of engineering experience, but still fail occasionally while providing relevancy. Don't they?

Further, the challenges of searching differ with the domain: the search on an e-commerce platform is about driving sales and bringing positive customer outcomes, whereas in fields such as medicine, it is about the matter of life and death. The lives of search engineers become more complicated because they do not have domain-specific knowledge, which can be used to understand the semantics of user queries.

However, despite of all the challenges, the implementation of search relevancy is up to you, and it depends on what information you can extract from the users, their queries, and the content they see. We continuously take feedback from users, create funnels, or enable loggings to capture the search behavior of users so that we can improve our algorithms to provide relevant results.

The Elasticsearch out-of-the-box tools

Elasticsearch primarily works with two models of information retrieval: the **Boolean model** and the **Vector Space model**. In addition to these, there are other scoring algorithms available in Elasticsearch as well, such as Okapi BM25, **Divergence from Randomness (DFR)**, and **Information Based (IB)**. Working with these three models requires extensive mathematical knowledge and needs some extra configurations in Elasticsearch, which are beyond the scope of this book.

The Boolean model uses the AND, OR, and NOT conditions in a query to find all the matching documents. This Boolean model can be further combined with the Lucene scoring formula, TF/IDF (which we have already discussed in *Chapter 2, Understanding Document Analysis and Creating Mappings*), to rank documents.

The vector space model works differently from the Boolean model, as it represents both queries and documents as vectors. In the vector space model, each number in the vector is the weight of a term that is calculated using TF/IDF.

The queries and documents are compared using a cosine similarity in which angles between two vectors are compared to find the similarity, which ultimately leads to finding the relevancy of the documents.

An example: why defaults are not enough

Let's build an index with sample documents to understand the examples in a better way.

First, create an index with the name `profiles`:

```
curl -XPUT 'localhost:9200/profiles'
```

Then, put the mapping with the document type as `candidate`:

```
curl -XPUT 'localhost:9200/profiles/candidate'

{
  "properties": {
    "geo_code": {
      "type": "geo_point",
      "lat_lon": true
    }
  }
}
```

Please note that in the preceding mapping, we are putting mapping only for the `geo` data type. The rest of the fields will be indexed dynamically.

Now, you can create a `data.json` file with the following content in it:

```
{ "index" : { "_index" : "profiles", "_type" : "candidate", "_id" : 1 }}
{ "name" : "Sam", "geo_code" : "12.9545163,77.3500487", "total_experience":5, "skills":["java","python"] }
{ "index" : { "_index" : "profiles", "_type" : "candidate", "_id" : 2 }}
{ "name" : "Robert", "geo_code" : "28.6619678,77.225706", "total_experience":2, "skills":["java"] }
{ "index" : { "_index" : "profiles", "_type" : "candidate", "_id" : 3 }}
{ "name" : "Lavleen", "geo_code" : "28.6619678,77.225706", "total_experience":4, "skills":["java","Elasticsearch"] }
{ "index" : { "_index" : "profiles", "_type" : "candidate", "_id" : 4 }}
{ "name" : "Bharvi", "geo_code" : "28.6619678,77.225706", "total_experience":3, "skills":["java","lucene"] }
{ "index" : { "_index" : "profiles", "_type" : "candidate", "_id" : 5 }}
{ "name" : "Nips", "geo_code" : "12.9545163,77.3500487", "total_experience":7, "skills":["grails","python"] }
{ "index" : { "_index" : "profiles", "_type" : "candidate", "_id" : 6 }}
{ "name" : "Shikha", "geo_code" : "28.4250666,76.8493508", "total_experience":10, "skills":["c","java"] }
```

If you are indexing skills, which are separated by spaces or which include non-English characters, that is, C++, C#, or Core Java, you need to create mapping for the `skills` field as `not_analyzed` in advance to have exact term matching.

Once the file is created, execute the following command to put the data inside the index we have just created:

```
curl -XPOST 'localhost:9200' --data-binary @data.json
```

If you look carefully at the example, the documents contain the data of the candidates who might be looking for jobs. For hiring candidates, a recruiter can have the following criteria:

- Candidates should know about Java
- Candidates should have experience of 3 to 5 years
- Candidates should fall in the distance range of 100 kilometers from the office of the recruiter

You can construct a simple `bool` query in combination with a term query on the `skills` field along with `geo_distance` and range filters on the `geo_code` and `total_experience` fields respectively. However, does this give a relevant set of results? The answer would be NO.

The problem is that if you are restricting the range of experience and distance, you might even get zero results or no suitable candidates. For example, you can put a range of 0 to 100 kilometers of distance but your perfect candidate might be at a distance of 101 kilometers. At the same time, if you define a wide range, you might get a huge number of non-relevant results.

The other problem is that if you search for candidates who know Java, there is a chance that a person who knows only Java and not any other programming language will be at the top, while a person who knows other languages apart from Java will be at the bottom. This happens because during the ranking of documents with TF/IDF, the lengths of the fields are taken into account. If the length of a field is small, the document is more relevant.

Elasticsearch is not intelligent enough to understand the semantic meaning of your queries, but for these scenarios, it offers you the full power to redefine how scoring and document ranking should be done.

Controlling relevancy with custom scoring

In most cases, you are good to go with the default scoring algorithms of Elasticsearch to return the most relevant results. However, some cases require you to have more control on the calculation of a score. This is especially required while implementing domain-specific logic such as finding the relevant candidates for a job, where you need to implement a very specific scoring formula. Elasticsearch provides you with the `function_score` query to take control of all these things.

 This chapter covers the code examples only in Java because a Python client gives you the flexibility to pass the query inside the body parameter of a search function as you have learned in the previous chapters. Python programmers can simply use the example queries in the same way. There is no extra module required to execute these queries. You can still download the Python code for this chapter from the Packt website.

The function_score query

The `function_score` query allows you to take the complete control of how a score needs to be calculated for a particular query.

The syntax of a `function_score` query:

```
{
  "query": {"function_score": {
    "query": {},
    "boost": "boost for the whole query",
    "functions": [
      {}
    ],
    "max_boost": number,
    "score_mode": "(multiply|max|...)",
    "boost_mode": "(multiply|replace|...)",
    "min_score" : number
  }}
}
```

The `function_score` query has two parts: the first is the base query that finds the overall pool of results you want. The second part is the list of functions, which are used to adjust the scoring. These functions can be applied to each document that matches the main query in order to alter or completely replace the original query `_score`.

In a `function_score` query, each function is composed of an optional filter that tells Elasticsearch which records should have their scores adjusted (this defaults to "all records") and a description of how to adjust the score.

The other parameters that can be used with a `functions_score` query are as follows:

- **boost**: An optional parameter that defines the boost for the entire query.

- **max_boost**: The maximum boost that will be applied by a function score.

- **boost_mode**: An optional parameter, which defaults to `multiply`. The `score` mode defines how the combined result of the score functions will influence the final score together with the subquery score. This can be `replace` (only the `function_score` is used; the query `score` is ignored), `max` (the maximum of the query score and the function score), `min` (the minimum of the query score and the function score), `sum` (the query score and the function score are added), `avg`, or `multiply` (the query score and the function score are multiplied).

- **score_mode**: This parameter specifies how the results of individual score functions will be aggregated. The possible values can be `first` (the first function that has a matching filter is applied), `avg`, `max`, `sum`, `min`, and `multiply`.

- **min_score**: The minimum score to be used.

 Excluding non-relevant documents with min_score
To exclude documents that do not meet a certain score threshold, the `min_score` parameter can be set to the desired score threshold.

The following are the built-in functions that are available to be used with the function score query:

- `weight`
- `field_value_factor`
- `script_score`
- The decay functions—`linear`, `exp`, and `gauss`

Let's see them one by one and then you will learn how to combine them in a single query.

weight

A `weight` function allows you to apply a simple boost to each document without the boost being normalized: a weight of 2 results in 2 * _score. For example:

```
GET profiles/candidate/_search
{
    "query": {
        "function_score": {
            "query": {
                "term": {
                    "skills": {
                        "value": "java"
                    }
                }
            },
            "functions": [
                {
                    "filter": {
                        "term": {
                            "skills": "python"
                        }
                    },
                    "weight": 2
                }
            ],
            "boost_mode": "replace"
        }
    }
}
```

The preceding query will match all the candidates who know Java, but will give a higher score to the candidates who also know Python. Please note that `boost_mode` is set to `replace`, which will cause _score to be calculated by a query that is to be overridden by the `weight` function for our particular filter clause. The query output will contain the candidates on top with a _score of 2 who know both Java and Python.

Java example:

The previous query can be implemented in Java in the following way:

1. First, you need to import the following classes into your code:

```
import org.elasticsearch.action.search.SearchResponse;
import org.elasticsearch.client.Client;
```

```
import org.elasticsearch.index.query.QueryBuilders;
import org.elasticsearch.index.query.functionscore.
FunctionScoreQueryBuilder;
import org.elasticsearch.index.query.functionscore.
ScoreFunctionBuilders;
```

2. Then the following code snippets can be used to implement the query:

```
FunctionScoreQueryBuilder functionQuery = new FunctionScoreQueryBu
ilder(QueryBuilders.termQuery("skills", "java"))

    .add(QueryBuilders.termQuery("skills", "python"),
ScoreFunctionBuilders.weightFactorFunction(2)).
boostMode("replace");


SearchResponse response =
client.prepareSearch().setIndices(indexName)
        .setTypes(docType).setQuery(functionQuery)
    .execute().actionGet();
```

field_value_factor

This uses the value of a field in the document to alter the _score:

```
GET profiles/candidate/_search
{
  "query": {
    "function_score": {
      "query": {
        "term": {
          "skills": {
            "value": "java"
          }
        }
      },
      "functions": [
        {
          "field_value_factor": {
            "field": "total_experience"
          }
        }
      ],
      "boost_mode": "multiply"
    }
  }
}
```

The preceding query finds all the candidates with Java in their skills, but influences the total score depending on the total experience of the candidate. So, the more experience the candidate has, the higher the ranking they will get. Please note that boost_mode is set to multiply, which will yield the following formula for the final scoring:

```
_score = _score * doc['total_experience'].value
```

However, there are two issues with the preceding approach: first is the documents that have the total experience value as 0 and will reset the final score to 0. Second, Lucene _score usually falls between 0 and 10, so a candidate with an experience of more than 10 years will completely swamp the effect of the full text search score.

To get rid of this problem, apart from using the field parameter, the field_value_factor function provides you with the following extra parameters to be used:

- factor: This is an optional factor to multiply the field value with. This defaults to 1.

- modifier: This is a mathematical modifier to apply to the field value. This can be: none, log, log1p, log2p, ln, ln1p, ln2p, square, sqrt, or reciprocal. It defaults to none.

Java example:

The preceding query can be implemented in Java in the following way:

1. First, you need to import the following classes into your code:

```
import org.elasticsearch.action.search.SearchResponse;
import org.elasticsearch.client.Client;
import org.elasticsearch.index.query.QueryBuilders;
import org.elasticsearch.index.query.functionscore*;
```

2. Then the following code snippets can be used to implement the query:

```
FunctionScoreQueryBuilder functionQuery = new FunctionScoreQueryBu
ilder(QueryBuilders.termQuery("skills", "java"))
    .add(new FieldValueFactorFunctionBuilder("total_experience")).
boostMode("multiply");

SearchResponse response = client.prepareSearch().
setIndices("profiles")
        .setTypes("candidate").setQuery(functionQuery)
        .execute().actionGet();
```

script_score

script_score is the most powerful function available in Elasticsearch. It uses a custom script to take complete control of the scoring logic. You can write a custom script to implement the logic you need. Scripting allows you to write from a simple to very complex logic. Scripts are cached, too, to allow faster executions of repetitive queries. Let's see an example:

```
{
  "script_score": {
    "script": "doc['total_experience'].value"
  }
}
```

Look at the special syntax to access the field values inside the script parameter. This is how the value of the fields is accessed using Groovy scripting language.

 Scripting is, by default, disabled in Elasticsearch, so to use script score functions, first you need to add this line in your elasticsearch.yml file: script.inline: on.

To see some of the power of this function, look at the following example:

```
GET profiles/candidate/_search
{
  "query": {
    "function_score": {
      "query": {
        "term": {
          "skills": {
            "value": "java"
          }
        }
      },
      "functions": [
        {
          "script_score": {
            "params": {
              "skill_array_provided": [
                "java",
                "python"
              ]
            },
```

```
        "script": "final_score=0; skill_array = doc['skills'].
toArray(); counter=0; while(counter<skill_array.size()){for(skill in
skill_array_provided){if(skill_array[counter]==skill){final_score =
final_score+doc['total_experience'].value};};counter=counter+1;};retu
rn final_score"
          }
        }
      ],
      "boost_mode": "replace"
    }
  }
}
```

Let's understand the preceding query:

- `params` is the placeholder where you can pass the parameters to your function, similar to how you use parameters inside a method signature in other languages. Inside the `script` parameter, you write your complete logic.

- This script iterates through each document that has Java mentioned in the skills, and for each document it fetches all the skills and stores them inside the `skill_array` variable. Finally, each skill that we have passed inside the `params` section is compared with the skills inside `skill_array`. If this matches, the value of the `final_score` variable is incremented with the value of the `total_experience` field of that document. The score calculated by the script score will be used to rank the documents because `boost_mode` is set to replace the original `_score` value.

Do not try to work with the analyzed fields while writing the scripts. You might get weird results. This is because, had our skills field contained a value such as "core java", you could not have got the exact matching for it inside the script section. So, the fields with space-separated values need to be set as `not_analyzed` or the keyword has to be analyzed in advance.

> To write these script functions, you need to have some command over groovy scripting. However, if you find it complex, you can write these scripts in other languages, such as Python, using the language plugin of Elasticsearch. More on this can be found here: `https://github.com/elastic/elasticsearch-lang-python`.
>
> For fast performance, use Groovy or Java functions. Python and JavaScript code requires the marshalling and unmarshalling of values that kill performance due to more CPU/memory usage.

Java example:

The previous query can be implemented in Java in the following way:

1. First, you need to import the following classes into your code:

    ```
    import org.elasticsearch.action.search.SearchResponse;
    import org.elasticsearch.client.Client;
    import org.elasticsearch.index.query.QueryBuilders;
    import org.elasticsearch.index.query.functionscore.*;
    import org.elasticsearch.script.Script;
    ```

2. Then, the following code snippets can be used to implement the query:

    ```
    String script = "final_score=0; skill_array =
    doc['skills'].toArray(); "
                    + "counter=0; while(counter<skill_array.size())"
                    + "{for(skill in skill_array_provided)"
                    + "{if(skill_array[counter]==skill)"
                    + "{final_score =      final_score+doc['total_experience'].
    value};};"
                    + "counter=counter+1;};return final_score";

    ArrayList<String> skills = new ArrayList<String>();
       skills.add("java");
       skills.add("python");

    Map<String, Object> params = new HashMap<String, Object>();
       params.put("skill_array_provided",skills);
       FunctionScoreQueryBuilder functionQuery = new

    FunctionScoreQueryBuilder(QueryBuilders.termQuery("skills",
    "java"))
         .add(new ScriptScoreFunctionBuilder(new Script(script,
    ScriptType.INLINE, "groovy", params))).boostMode("replace");

    SearchResponse response =    client.prepareSearch().
    setIndices(indexName)
             .setTypes(docType).setQuery(functionQuery)
             .execute().actionGet();
    ```

As you can see, the script logic is a simple string that is used to instantiate the `Script` class constructor inside `ScriptScoreFunctionBuilder`.

Decay functions - linear, exp, and gauss

We have seen the problems of restricting the range of experience and distance that could result in getting zero results or no suitable candidates. Maybe a recruiter would like to hire a candidate from a different province because of a good candidate profile. So, instead of completely restricting with the range filters, we can incorporate sliding-scale values such as geo_location or dates into _score to prefer documents near a latitude/longitude point or recently published documents.

function_score provide to work with this sliding scale with the help of three decay functions: linear, exp (that is, exponential), and gauss (that is, Gaussian). All three functions take the same parameter, as shown in the following code and are required to control the shape of the curve created for the decay function: origin, scale, decay, and offset.

The point of origin is used to calculate distance. For date fields, the default is the current timestamp. The scale parameter defines the distance from the origin at which the computed score will be equal to the decay parameter.

The origin and scale parameters can be thought of as your min and max that define a bounding box within which the curve will be defined. If we wanted to give more boosts to the documents that have been published in the past 10 days, it would be best to define the origin as the current timestamp and the scale as 10d.

The offset specifies that the decay function will only compute the decay function of documents with a distance greater that the defined offset. The default is 0.

Finally, the decay option alters how severely the document is demoted based on its position. The default decay value is 0.5.

> All three decay functions work only on numeric, date, and geo-point fields.

```
GET profiles/candidate/_search
{
  "query": {
    "function_score": {
      "query": {
        "match_all": {}
      },
      "functions": [
        {
          "exp": {
            "geo_code": {
```

```
                    "origin": {
                      "lat": 28.66,
                      "lon": 77.22
                    },
                    "scale": "100km"
                }
              }
            }
        ],"boost_mode": "multiply"
      }
    }
  }
}
```

In the preceding query, we have used the exponential decay function that tells Elasticsearch to start decaying the score calculation after a distance of 100 km from the given origin. So, the candidates who are at a distance of greater than 100 km from the given origin will be ranked low, but not discarded. These candidates can still get a higher rank if we combine other function score queries such as weight or `field_value_factor` with the decay function and combine the result of all the functions together.

Java example:

The preceding query can be implemented in Java in the following way:

1. First, you need to import the following classes into your code:
   ```
   import org.elasticsearch.action.search.SearchResponse;
   import org.elasticsearch.client.Client;
   import org.elasticsearch.index.query.QueryBuilders;
   import org.elasticsearch.index.query.functionscore.*;
   ```

2. Then, the following code snippets can be used to implement the query:
   ```
   Map<String, Object> origin = new HashMap<String, Object>();
       String scale = "100km";
       origin.put("lat", "28.66");
       origin.put("lon", "77.22");
   FunctionScoreQueryBuilder functionQuery = new
       FunctionScoreQueryBuilder()
       .add(new ExponentialDecayFunctionBuilder("geo_code",origin,
       scale)).boostMode("multiply");
   //For Linear Decay Function use below syntax
   //.add(new LinearDecayFunctionBuilder("geo_code",origin,
     scale)).boostMode("multiply");
   //For Gauss Decay Function use below syntax
   ```

```
//.add(new GaussDecayFunctionBuilder("geo_code",origin,
  scale)).boostMode("multiply");

SearchResponse response =
client.prepareSearch().setIndices(indexName)
        .setTypes(docType).setQuery(functionQuery)
        .execute().actionGet();
```

In the preceding example, we have used the exp decay function but, the commented lines show examples of how other decay functions can be used.

Last, as always, remember that Elasticsearch lets you use multiple functions in a single function_score query to calculate a score that combines the results of each function.

Summary

This chapter covered the most important aspects of search engines; that is, relevancy. We discussed the powerful scoring capabilities available in Elasticsearch and the practical examples to show how you can control the scoring process according to your needs. Despite the relevancy challenges faced while working with search engines, the out-of-the-box features such as function scores and custom scoring always allow us to tackle challenges with ease.

In the next chapter, you will learn how to set up an Elasticsearch cluster and configure different types of node for production deployments.

9
Cluster Scaling in Production Deployments

Until now, we have been more focused about the search and data analytics capabilities of Elasticsearch. Now is the time to learn about taking Elasticsearch clusters in production while focusing on best practices.

In this chapter, we will cover the following topics:

- Node types in Elasticsearch
- Introducing Zen-Discovery
- Best Elasticsearch practices in production
- Cluster creation
- Scaling your clusters

Node types in Elasticsearch

In Elasticsearch, you can configure three types of nodes, as shown in the following cluster:

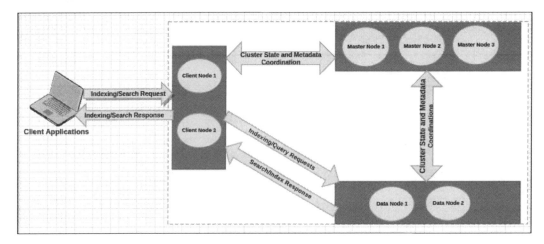

In the preceding cluster diagram, there are two client nodes, three master nodes, and two data nodes. Let's understand how these node types differ in Elasticsearch and how to configure them.

Client node

A client node in Elasticsearch acts as a query router and a load balancer. It does not hold any data. A client node can be used to query as well as index processes. It takes queries and distributes the search to data nodes. Once the data nodes return their respective results, the client node combines all the data to give the final results. Similarly, when you send the data to a client node for indexing, it calculates the sharding key for each document and sends the documents for the respective shards.

A client node can be configured by adding the following lines to the `elasticsearch.yml` file:

- `node.data: false`
- `node.master: false`

Data node

A data node in the Elasticsearch is responsible for holding the data, merging segments, and executing queries. Data nodes are the real work horses of your cluster and need a higher configuration than any other type of node in the cluster.

A data node can be configured by adding the following lines to the `elasticsearch.yml` file:

- `node.data: true`
- `node.master: false`

Master node

A master node is responsible for the management of the complete cluster. It holds the states of all the nodes and periodically distributes the cluster state to all the other nodes in the cluster to make them aware of any new node that has joined the cluster and which nodes have left. A master node periodically sends a ping to all the other nodes to see whether they are alive (other nodes also send pings to the master node). The final major task of the master node is configuration management. It holds the complete meta-data and the mapping of all the indexes in the cluster. If a master leaves, a new master node is chosen from the rest of the master-eligible nodes. If there is no master-eligible node left, the cluster cannot operate at all.

A master node can be configured by adding the following lines to the `elasticsearch.yml` file.

- `node.data: false`
- `node.master: true`

> By default, every node is configured as node.data: true and node. master: true, which means every node is a data node and can also act as a master node.

Introducing Zen-Discovery

Elasticsearch is highly scalable and distributed in nature. This scalability would not have been possible without a reliable centralized co-ordination system. In fact, every distributed system requires a coordination system to maintain configuration information' and provide distributed synchronizations to all the nodes connected in the cluster. If you have worked with SolrCloud, you will know that it uses a coordination service known as **Zookeeper**. Zookeeper is an awesome open source project as a whole and can be used with many distributed systems, even with Elasticsearch by installing the plugin.

At the heart of Elasticsearch, there is no third-party coordination service. However, Elasticsearch does have a built-in centralized coordination mechanism—**Zen Discovery**. One of the primary tasks of Discovery is to choose a master node that looks after the entire cluster.

When you start a node in an Elasticsearch cluster, the first thing that happens is that a node searches for the master node that has the same cluster name. If it finds one, it simply joins the cluster, and if there is no master node available and this newly started node is master eligible (we will see what it means), then it becomes the master node. This process of cluster formation is known as discovery.

Zen-Discovery allows you to have two types of discovery mechanisms: **Multicasting** and **Unicasting**.

Multicasting discovery

In the versions before 2.0, mulitcast used to be the default discovery type in Elasticsearch. However, since version 2.0, this has been changed to unicast discovery.

The reason was that multicasting is good to go in a development environment, but comes with added disadvantages. In multicasting, every node in the cluster sends message packets to all the other nodes for communication and health checks. This not only makes the network congested because of too many message transmissions in the network, it also makes it less secure. Any node that is unwanted and has the same cluster name can automatically join the cluster.

To enable the multicasting discovery type, add the following parameter in all the nodes of your cluster and restart them:

- `discovery.zen.ping.multicast.enabled: true`

Unicasting discovery

In unicasting discovery, the transmission of a single message is sent over the network to a single host at once. Here, you configure a set of nodes that can receive the messages from the node that wants to join the cluster. The unicasting mechanism is secure too since a node that wants to join the cluster must know the address and port of the master nodes that are responsible for deciding who will join the cluster.

Configuring unicasting discovery

To configure unicasting discovery, there are four properties that need to be configured inside the `elasticsearch.yml` file.

Minimum number of master nodes: preventing split-brain

A split-brain is the situation in which one Elasticsearch cluster divides itself into two clusters, and each cluster has a separate master node. This is mainly caused by network issues or when a cluster becomes unstable because nodes experience long pauses due to slow garbage collections. The subsets of nodes attempt to form their own clusters, and this is known as a **Split-Brain** situation. In this situation, the nodes are diverged and cannot form a single cluster again until you kill the other half of the cluster. Split-brain can be very dangerous and can incur potential data loss. Luckily, the Elasticsearch team has worked hard to prevent the worst scenarios of handling split-brain situations, but the implementation is up to you.

To avoid split-brain, you need to decide the minimum number of master nodes that must be operational in the cluster to keep the cluster running. The size of the minimum number of master nodes depends on the total number of master nodes you have in your cluster. It can be set using the `discovery.zen.minimum_master_nodes` property inside the `elasticsearch.yml` file:

- `discovery.zen.minimum_master_nodes: n`

Here, n is the integer value of the minimum number of master nodes. As per recommendation, this value should be decided based on the formula, *N/2+1*, where N is the total number of master nodes in the cluster. So, if you have three master nodes, this parameter can be set as *3/2+1 = 2* (rounding off to the nearest integer).

An initial list of hosts to ping

Unicasting requires an initial list of hosts to be pinged when a new node is started to form a cluster. Here you need to provide the list of all your master nodes along with an optional TCP port number in the following format:

```
discovery.zen.ping.unicast.hosts: ["masternode1IPAddress:TCP-
Port","masternode2IPAddress:TCP-Port", "masternode3IPAddress:TCP-
Port"]
```

The TCP port defaults to 9300.

Ping timeout

This, by default, has 3s; within this time the nodes will ping to the master node and the master node will ping back to the other nodes to ensure that all nodes are up. This property should be set to a higher value in a slow network or a congested cluster. It can be configured in the following way:

- `discovery.zen.ping.timeout: 5s`

Node upgrades without downtime

To achieve SLAs, you need highly available systems. However, at the same time, you may need to upgrade or downgrade your machines or even upgrade Elasticsearch to its upgraded release. Both cases require some best practices to be followed because one wrong step can incur data loss or a delay in the completion of the required changes. In both the cases, one thing is for sure, nodes must be stopped one by one. While it's easy to stop the client or the master node and perform maintenance tasks, data nodes require special considerations because they might need a higher shard recovery time.

Every time a data node is restarted, shard re-balancing is done by Elasticsearch, which takes too much time because of some unnecessary data movement and synchronization inside the cluster. To avoid this scenario and for a faster recovery of the data nodes, follow these steps.

Before stopping a data node, set the shard routing allocation to none with the following command:

```
PUT _cluster/settings
{
"transient" : {
"cluster.routing.allocation.enable" : "none"
}
}
```

After starting the data node, set back the shard routing allocation to all with this command:

```
PUT _cluster/settings
{
"transient" : {
"cluster.routing.allocation.enable" : "all"
}
}
```

An Elasticsearch version can't be downgraded to a lower release. So, take data backups before going for a version upgrade. Backup and restores are covered in the next chapter.

Upgrading Elasticsearch version

An Elasticsearch cluster can be upgraded to a higher version in two ways:

- **Rolling upgrade**: This requires one node to stop at once and perform the upgradation.

- **Full cluster restart**: This requires a complete cluster shutdown before proceeding with the upgrade task.

You need to go through the following URL for more information on the supported versions to choose the type of upgrade you need to perform:

https://www.elastic.co/guide/en/elasticsearch/reference/current/setup-upgrade.html

In both cases, to upgrade a node, the following are the easiest steps to upgrade a version node by node:

1. Disable the routing allocation, as discussed in the previous section.
2. Stop the node.
3. Take a backup of the data.
4. Take a backup of the configuration files.
5. Remove Elasticsearch (you can simply purge it to complete the uninstallation of Elasticsearch from the server by running this command: `sudo apt-get purge Elasticsearch`)
6. Install Elasticsearch with the latest release.
7. Change the configuration files according to the previous settings.
8. Upgrade the plugins.
9. Restart the node.

Best Elasticsearch practices in production

This section is dedicated to guide you on following the best practices and considerations to keep in mind when going into production.

Memory

- Always choose ES_HEAP_SIZE 50% of the total available memory. Sorting and aggregations both can be memory hungry, so enough heap space to accommodate these is required. This property is set inside the `/etc/init.d/elasticsearch` file.

- A machine with 64 GB of RAM is ideal; however, 32 GB and 16 GB machines are also common. Less than 8 GB tends to be counterproductive (you end up needing smaller machines), and greater than 64 GB has problems in pointer compression.

CPU

Choose a modern processor with multiple cores. If you need to choose between faster CPUs or more cores, choose more cores. The extra concurrency that multiple cores offer will far outweigh a slightly faster clock speed. The number of threads is dependent on the number of cores. The more cores you have, the more threads you get for indexing, searching, merging, bulk, or other operations.

Disks

- If you can afford SSDs, they are far superior to any spinning media. SSD-backed nodes see boosts in both querying and indexing performance.

- Avoid network-attached storage (NAS) to store data.

Network

- The faster the network you have, the more performance you will get in a distributed system. Low latency helps to ensure that nodes communicate easily, while a high bandwidth helps in shard movement and recovery.

- Avoid clusters that span multiple data centers even if the data centers are collocated in close proximity. Definitely avoid clusters that span large geographic distances.

General consideration

- It is better to prefer medium-to-large boxes. Avoid small machines because you don't want to manage a cluster with a thousand nodes, and the overhead of simply running Elasticsearch is more apparent on such small boxes.

- Always use a Java version greater than JDK1.7 Update 55 from Oracle and avoid using Open JDK.

- A master node does not require much resources. In a cluster with 2 Terabytes of data having 100s of indexes, 2 GB of RAM, 1 Core CPU, and 10 GB of disk space is good enough for the master nodes. In the same scenario, the client nodes with 8 GB of RAM each and 2 Core CPUs is a very good configuration to handle millions of requests. The configuration of data nodes is completely dependent on the speed of indexing, the type of queries, and aggregations. However, they usually need very high configurations such as 64 GB of RAM and 8 Core CPUs.

Some other important configuration changes

- Assign Names: Assign the cluster name and node name.
- Assign Paths: Assign the log path and data path.
- Recovery Settings: Avoid shard shuffles during recovery. The recovery throttling section should be tweaked in large clusters only; otherwise, it comes with very good defaults.

  Disable the deletion of all the indices by a single command:

  ```
  action.disable_delete_all_indices: false
  ```

- Ensure by setting the following property that you do not run more than one Elasticsearch instance from a single installation:

  ```
  max_local_storage_nodes: "1"
  ```

  Disable HTTP requests on all the data and master nodes in the following way:

  ```
  http.enabled: false
  ```

- Plugins installations: Always prefer to install the compatible plugin version according to the Elasticsearch version you are using and after the installation of the plugin, do not forget to restart the node.

- Avoid storing Marvel indexes in the production cluster.

- Clear the cache if the heap fills up when the node start-up and shards refuse to get initialized after going into red state This can be done by executing the following command:

    ◦ To clear the cache of the complete cluster:

    ```
    curl -XPOST 'http://localhost:9200/_cache/clear'
    ```

    ◦ To clear the cache of a single index:

    ```
    curl -XPOST 'http://localhost:9200/index_name/_cache/clear'
    ```

- Use routing wherever beneficial for faster indexing and querying.

Creating a cluster

Since you have learned a major part of cluster configuration, let's begin to create a full-blown production-ready cluster. In this example, we will configure a cluster with three master, two client nodes, and two data nodes.

The example shows a configuration of one master, one data, and one client node. On the rest of nodes, all the configuration will remain the same according to the node category, but only four parameters will be changed:

`node.name`, `path.data`, `path.log` and `network.host`.

 If you are configuring a new data or log path, make sure that Elasticsearch has the full permission of that directory. You can set the permission with the following command:

```
sudo chown -R elasticsearch:elasticsearch
path_of_the_data_directory
```

Configuring master nodes

```
cluster.name: "production-cluster"
node.name: "es-master-01"
node.data: false
node.master: true
path.data: "path_to_data_directory"
network.host: "192.168.1.10" (should be changed to a private IP
address of this machine or can be left out too, because Elasticsearch,
by default, binds itself to the 0.0.0.0 address)
http.enabled: false
transport.tcp.port: 9300
```

```
discovery.zen.minimum_master_nodes: 3
discovery.zen.ping.unicast.hosts: ["es-master-01:6300","es-
master-02:6300", "es-master-03:6300"]
discovery.zen.ping.timeout: 5s
bootstrap.mlockall: true
action.destructive_requires_name: true
#For allowing script execution
script.inline: on
```

Configuring client nodes

```
cluster.name: "production-cluster"
node.name: "es-client-01"
node.data: false
node.master: false
network.host: "192.168.1.10" (should be changed to the private IP
address of this machine)
http.enabled: true
http.port: 9200
transport.tcp.port: 9300
discovery.zen.minimum_master_nodes: 3
discovery.zen.ping.unicast.hosts: ["es-master-01:9300","es-
master-02:9300", "es-master-03:9300"]
discovery.zen.ping.timeout: 5s
bootstrap.mlockall: true
action.destructive_requires_name: true
action.disable_delete_all_indices: false
script.inline: on
#To allow sense and marvel to query elasticsearch
http.cors.enabled: true
http.cors.allow-origin: /http:\/\/localhost(:[0-9]+)?/
http.cors.allow-credentials: true
```

Configuring data nodes

```
cluster.name: "production-cluster"
node.name: "es-data-01"
node.data: true
node.master: false
network.host: "192.168.1.10" (should be changed to the private IP
address of this machine)
http.enabled: false
transport.tcp.port: 9300
discovery.zen.minimum_master_nodes: 3
```

```
discovery.zen.ping.unicast.hosts: ["es-master-01:9300","es-
master-02:9300", "es-master-03:9300"]
discovery.zen.ping.timeout: 5s
bootstrap.mlockall: true
action.destructive_requires_name: true
script.inline: on
```

Scaling your clusters

While it's easy to get started with the launching of nodes and the forming of Elasticsearch clusters, the real challenge comes when the indexing and searching requests increase and your server encounters real pressure. In this section, we will discuss when and how to scale your Elasticsearch clusters.

 Cluster scaling is only possible if you have done some capacity planning in advance and have decided on an optimal number of shards. Always remember that once an index is created, you cannot increase or decrease the number of shards but can always change the number of replicas.

When to scale

Elasticsearch is very good at giving you hints in advance when it starts getting overloaded. The problems can arise in many areas such as slow searches, disk space utilizations, JVM issues, memory pressure, or high CPU utilizations. In any case, scaling should be done before your servers crash.

For timely scaling, the best thing to do is keep a close eye on the monitoring of the metrics provided by Elasticsearch for all resource utilizations. Your biggest friend would be Marvel. It provides very granular statistics of your clusters. However, in case you can't opt for **Marvel** due to any reason, you can use a combination of three approaches: use monitoring plugins such as `Bigdesk`, `HQ`; keep watching the logs and use the monitoring REST APIs to get a clear idea of what is causing the problem; and taking decisions about when to scale.

Metrics to watch

The following are the most important metrics that you need to continuously watch out for in Elasticsearch.

CPU utilization

The performance of Elasticsearch is highly dependent on the type of server on which it has been installed. There are many reasons for spikes in high CPU utilizations, such as higher indexing speed that causes a lot of segment merges in the background or higher garbage collection activities. Look at the following images that have been taken after running the `htop` command on a Ubuntu system:

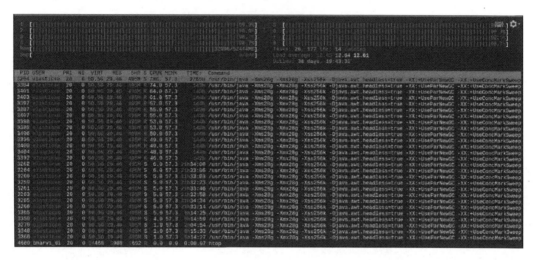

The preceding screenshot is from my server, which has eight CPU cores and 32 GB of RAM (16 GB dedicated to Elasticsearch). You can see Elasticsearch is using almost 800% of CPU because of a higher indexing rate of almost 3,000 documents per second (with a size of 20 KB per document). We were required to increase the indexing rate, but we were not able to because there was no room in the CPU.

The only solution in this scenario was to scale, either vertically (increasing CPU of this server) or horizontally (adding more nodes to allocate some of the shards on a new node), to distribute the load.

The same CPU utilization can be viewed with the help of the `Bigdesk` plugin:

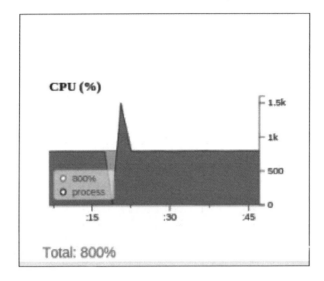

Memory utilization

Elasticsearch is a memory extensive process. It runs in JVM and requires a lot of memory holding objects while performing aggregation, sorting, and caching different kinds of data, such as field cache and filter cache, to give you faster search executions. Many people are worried when they see that Elasticsearch is using almost all the memory of the server. However, this is not always correct. In Elasticsearch, it is good if your server is utilizing all the memory. The actual thing to look for is whether there is any free buffer or cached memory available.

When there is too much memory pressure on an Elasticsearch node, it starts giving warnings in the logs of that particular node, similar to the following one:

```
[2015-11-25 18:13:53,166] [WARN ] [monitor.jvm] [es-data-1] [gc] [ParNew]
[1135087] [11248] duration [2.6m], collections [1]/[2.7m], total [2.6m]/
[6.8m], memory [2.4gb]->[2.3gb]/[3.8gb], all_pools {[Code Cache]
[13.7mb]->[13.7mb]/[48mb]}{[Par Eden Space] [109.6mb]->[15.4mb]/[1gb]}
{[Par Survivor Space] [136.5mb]->[0b]/[136.5mb]}{[CMS Old Gen] [2.1gb]-
>[2.3gb]/[2.6gb]}{[CMS Perm Gen] [35.1mb]->[34.9mb]/[82mb]}
```

If you start getting these kinds of warnings in your logs, its time to add more resources.

Disk I/O utilization

If you are working on applications having high writes such as logging and real-time data indexing, you need very high disk I/Ops. Elasticsearch provides options for tuning store-level throttling for segment merging; however, spinning media disks cannot cope with heavy writes. It is best to use SSD for write heavy applications. In our applications, we have seen an almost 10x performance boost after opting for SSD.

Disk low watermark

Look at the following lines of log, which have been taken from the master node of the cluster:

```
[2015-11-21 15:22:52,656][INFO ][cluster.routing.allocation.decider] [es-master-1] low disk watermark [15%] exceeded on [ujhOO-MzR22bJHPUGLtyQA] [es-data-1] free: 36.6gb[14.8%], replicas will not be assigned to this node
```

It clearly says that one of the data nodes has less than 15% of disk space available and new shards won't be assigned to this node anymore. This can even be worse if 90% of the disk is full. In this case, your shards will be automatically assigned to other nodes, and if the other nodes also have the same disk space, your cluster will go into hang mode.

However, you can increase the thresholds for low and high watermarks in the following way:

```
curl -XPUT client_node_ip:9200/_cluster/settings -d '{
    "transient" : {

        "cluster.routing.allocation.disk.watermark.low" : "90%",
        "cluster.routing.allocation.disk.watermark.high" : "10gb"
    }
}'
```

As you can see, these parameters take values in the form of percentage as well as gigabytes or megabytes. However, if this is still not enough, you need to add more nodes to move the shards or increase the disk space.

How to scale

Distributed systems such as Elasticsearch, Cassandra, or Mongodb are built for higher scalability. However, it is very important to consider one thing: how you scale your clusters. Scaling can be done either vertically or horizontally. Vertical scaling is the one in which you keep adding more resources to existing machines, whereas in horizontal scaling, you dynamically add more nodes to the cluster. Elasticsearch is built for horizontal scaling. You keep adding more nodes to your cluster, and it can automatically balance the shards/load on the new nodes.

To add new nodes to Elasticsearch, simply launch a new server with Elasticsearch installed on it and similar configuration (cluster name and discovery parameters). It will automatically connect to the existing cluster, if it is able to connect with your master nodes.

There are still some scenarios in which it will be required to go for vertical scaling, such as cost optimizations. In this case, you need to stop the node and increase the resources on it. However, you need to have enough nodes to keep the cluster operational, such as having two client nodes or two data nodes and three master nodes.

Summary

In this chapter, you learned how to configure different types of nodes in Elasticsearch, along with keeping best practices in mind when going for the production deployments of an Elasticsearch cluster. The chapter covered one of the most important aspects of cluster sizing – resource allocation and configuration for different types of nodes.

Finally, we saw some key metrics such as CPU, disk I/Ops, RAM, and utilizations to watch out for when your cluster needs scaling and the best practices to follow for scaling without downtime.

In the next chapter, we will learn about securing clusters and creating data backups.

10
Backups and Security

Data backups and data security are the most important aspects of any organization. It is even more important to design and implement business continuity plans to tackle data loss because of various factors. While Elasticsearch is not a database and it does not provide the backup and security functionalities that you can get in databases, it still offers some way around this. Let's learn how you can create cost effective and robust backup plans for your Elasticsearch clusters.

In this chapter, we will cover the following topics:

- Introducing backup and restore mechanisms
- Securing an Elasticsearch cluster
- Load balancing using Nginx

Introducing backup and restore mechanisms

In Elasticsearch, you can implement a backup and restore functionality in two different ways depending on the requirements and efforts put in. You can either create a script to create manual backups and restoration or you can opt for a more automated and functionality-rich **Backup-Restore** API offered by Elasticsearch.

Backup using snapshot API

A snapshot is the backup of a complete cluster or selected indices. The best thing about snapshots is that they are incremental in nature. So, only data that has been changed since the last snapshot will be taken in the next snapshot.

Life was not so easy before the release of Elasticsearch Version 1.0.0. This release not only introduced powerful aggregation functionalities to Elasticsearch, but also brought in the **Snapshot Restore** API to create backups and restore them on the fly. Initially, only a shared file system was supported by this API, but gradually it has been possible to use this API on AWS to create backups on AWS buckets, Hadoop to create backups inside Hadoop clusters, and Microsoft Azure to create backups on **Azure Storage** with the help of plugins. In the upcoming section, you will learn how to create backups using a shared file system repository. To use cloud and Hadoop plugins, have a look at the following URLs:

```
https://github.com/elastic/elasticsearch-cloud-aws#s3-repository
```

```
https://github.com/elastic/elasticsearch-hadoop/tree/master/
repository-hdfs
```

```
https://github.com/elastic/elasticsearch-cloud-azure#azure-repository
```

Creating snapshots using file system repositories requires the repository to be accessible from all the data and master nodes in the cluster. For this, we will be creating an **network file system** (**NFS**) drive in the next section.

Creating an NFS drive

NFS is a distributed file system protocol, which allows you to mount remote directories on your server. The mounted directories look like the local directory of the server, therefore using NFS, multiple servers can write to the same directory.

Let's take an example to create a shared directory using NFS. For this example, there is one host server, which can also be viewed as a backup server of Elasticsearch data, two data nodes, and three master nodes.

The following are the IP addresses of all these nodes:

- Host Server: 10.240.131.44
- Data node 1: 10.240.251.58
- Data node 1: 10.240.251.59
- Master Node 1: 10.240.80.41
- Master Node 2: 10.240.80.42
- Master Node 3: 10.240.80.43

Configuring the NFS host server

The very first step is to install the `nfs-kernel-server` package after updating the local package index:

```
sudo apt-get update
sudo apt-get install nfs-kernel-server
```

Once the package is installed, you can create a directory that can be shared among all the clients. Let's create a directory:

```
sudo mkdir /mnt/shared-directory
```

Give the access permission of this directory to the **nobody** user and the **nogroup** group. They are a special reserved user and group in the Linux operating system that do not need any special permission to run things:

```
sudo chown -R nobody:nogroup /mnt/shared-directory
```

The next step is to configure the **NFS Exports**, where we can specify with which machine this directory will be shared. For this, open the `/etc/exports` file with root permissions:

```
sudo nano /etc/exports
```

Add the following line, which contains the directory to be shared and the space-separated client IP lists:

```
/mnt/shared-directory    10.240.251.58(rw,sync,no_subtree_check)
10.240.251.59(rw,sync,no_subtree_check) 10.240.80.41(rw,sync,no_subtree_
check) 10.240.80.42(rw,sync,no_subtree_check) 10.240.80.43(rw,sync,no_
subtree_check)
```

Once done, save the file and exit.

The next step is to create an NFS table, which holds the exports of your share by running the following command:

```
sudo exportfs -a
```

Now start the NFS service by running this command:

```
sudo service nfs-kernel-server start
```

After this, your shared directory is available to the clients you have configured on your host machine. It's time to do the configurations on the client machines.

Configuring client machines

First of all, your need to install the NFS client after updating the local package index:

```
sudo apt-get update
sudo apt-get install nfs-common
```

Now, create a directory on the client machine that will be used to mount the remote shared directory:

```
sudo mkdir /mnt/nfs
```

Mount the shared directory (by specifying the nfs server host ip:shared directory name) on the client machine by using the following command:

```
sudo mount 10.240.131.44:/mnt/shared-directory /mnt/nfs
```

To check whether the mount is successfully done, you can use the following command:

```
df -h
```

You will see an extra drive mounted on your system, as shown in the following screenshot, which shows the mounted shared directory:

```
bharvi@es-master-1:~$ df -h
Filesystem                                        Size  Used Avail Use% Mounted on
rootfs                                            9.8G  1.4G  7.9G  16% /
udev                                               10M     0   10M   0% /dev
tmpfs                                             171M  148K  171M   1% /run
/dev/disk/by-uuid/906181f7-4e10-4a4e-8fd8-43b20ec980ff  9.8G  1.4G  7.9G  16% /
tmpfs                                             5.0M     0  5.0M   0% /run/lock
tmpfs                                             341M     0  341M   0% /run/shm
10.240.131.44:/mnt/shared-directory              9.8G   23M  9.2G   1% /mnt/nfs
```

Please note that mounting the directories/devices using the mount command only mounts them temporarily. For a permanent mount, open the /etc/fstab file:

```
sudo nano /etc/fstab
```

Add these lines to this file:

```
host.domain.com:/mnt/shared-directory    /mnt/nfs/    nfs auto,noatime,nol
ock,bg,nfsvers=4,sec=krb5p,intr,tcp,actimeo=1800 0 0
```

Perform similar steps on all the data and master nodes to mount the shared directory on all of them using NFS.

Creating a snapshot

The following subsections cover the various steps that are performed to create
a snapshot.

Registering the repository path

Add the following line inside the `elasticsearch.yml` file, to register the `path.repo`
setting on all the master and data nodes:

```
path.repo: ["/mnt/nfs"]
```

After this, restart the nodes one by one to reload the configuration.

Registering the shared file system repository in Elasticsearch

Register the shared file system repository with the name `es-backup`:

```
curl -XPUT 'http://localhost:9200/_snapshot/es-backup' -d '{
    "type": "fs",
    "settings": {
        "location": "/mnt/nfs/es-backup",
        "compress": true
    }
}'
```

In preceding request, the `location` parameter specifies the path of the snapshots and
the `compress` parameter turns on the compression of the snapshot files. Compression
is applied only to the index metadata files (mappings and settings) and not to the
data files.

Create your first snapshot

You can create multiple snapshots of the same cluster within a repository.
The following is the command that is used to create a `snapshot_1` snapshot
inside the `es-snapshot` repository:

```
curl -XPUT 'http://localhost:9200/_snapshot/es-backup/snapshot_1?wait_
for_completion=true'
```

The `wait_for_completion` parameter tells whether the request should return
immediately after snapshot initialization (defaults to true) or wait for snapshot
completion. During snapshot initialization, information about all previous
snapshots is loaded into the memory, which means that in large repositories,
it may take several seconds (or even minutes) for this command to return even
if the `wait_for_completion` parameter is set to false.

By default, a snapshot of all the open and started indices in the cluster is created. This behavior can be changed by specifying the list of indices in the body of the snapshot request:

```
curl -XPUT 'http://localhost:9200/_snapshot/es-backup/snapshot_1?wait_
for_completion=true' -d '{
  "indices": "index_1,index_2",
  "ignore_unavailable": "true",
  "include_global_state": false
}'
```

In the preceding request, the indices parameter specifies the names of the indices that need to be included inside the snapshot. The ignore_unavailable parameter, if set to true, enables a snapshot request to not fail if any index is not available in the snapshot creation request. The third parameter, include_global_state, when set to false, avoids the global cluster state to be stored as a part of the snapshot.

Getting snapshot information

To get the details of a single snapshot, you can run the following command:

```
curl -XPUT 'http://localhost:9200/_snapshot /es-backup/snapshot_1
```

Use comma-separated snapshot names to get the details of more than one snapshot:

```
curl -XPUT 'http://localhost:9200/_snapshot /es-backup/snapshot_1
```

To get the details of all the snapshots, use _all in the end, like this:

```
curl -XPUT 'http://localhost:9200/_snapshot /es-backup/_all
```

Deleting snapshots

A snapshot can be deleted using the following command:

```
curl -XDELETE 'http://localhost:9200/_snapshot /es-backup/snapshot_1
```

Restoring snapshots

Restoring a snapshot is very easy and a snapshot can be restored to other clusters too, provided the cluster in which you are restoring is version compatible. You cannot restore a snapshot to a lower version of Elasticsearch.

While restoring snapshots, if the index does not already exist, a new index will be created with the same index name and all the mappings for that index, which was there before creating the snapshot. If the index already exists, then it must be in the closed state and must have the same number of shards as the index snapshot. The restore operation automatically opens the indexes after a successful completion:

Example: restoring a snapshot

To take an example of restoring a snapshot from the `es-backup` repository and the `snapshot_1` snapshot, run the following command against the `_restore` endpoint on the client node:

```
curl -XPOST localhost:9200/_snapshot/es-backup/snapshot_1/_restore
```

This command will restore all the indices of the snapshot.

Elasticsearch offers several options while restoring the snapshots. The following are some of the important ones.

Restoring multiple indices

There might be a scenario in which you do not want to restore all the indices of a snapshot and only a few indices. For this, you can use the following command:

```
curl -XPOST 'localhost:9200/_snapshot/es-backup/snapshot_1/_restore' -d
'{
  "indices": "index_1,index_2",
  "ignore_unavailable": "true"
}'
```

Renaming indices

Elasticsearch does not have any option to rename an index once it has been created, apart from setting aliases. However, it provides you with an option to rename the indices while restoring from the snapshot. For example:

```
curl -XPOST 'localhost:9200/_snapshot/es-backup/snapshot_1/_restore' -d
'{
  "indices": "index_1",
  "ignore_unavailable": "true",
  "rename_replacement": "restored_index"
}'
```

Partial restore

Partial restore is a very useful feature. It comes in handy in scenarios such as creating snapshots, if the snapshots can not be created for some of the shards. In this case, the entire restore process will fail if one or more indices does not have a snapshot of all the shards. In this case, you can use the following command to restore such indices back into cluster:

```
curl -XPOST 'localhost:9200/_snapshot/es-backup/snapshot_1/_restore' -d
'{
  "partial": true
}'
```

Note that you will lose the data of the missing shard in this case, and those missing shards will be created as empty ones after the completion of the restore process.

Changing index settings during restore

During restoration, many of the index settings can be changed, such as the number of replicas and refresh intervals. For example, to restore an index named my_index with a replica size of 0 (for a faster restore process) and a default refresh interval rate, you can run this command:

```
curl -XPOST 'localhost:9200/_snapshot/es-backup/snapshot_1/_restore' -d
'{
  "indices": "my_index",
  "index_settings": {
    "index.number_of_replicas": 0
  },
  "ignore_index_settings": [
    "index.refresh_interval"
  ]
}'
```

The indices parameter can contain more than one comma separated index_name.

Once restored, the replicas can be increased with the following command:

```
curl -XPUT 'localhost:9200/my_index/_settings' -d '
{
    "index" : {
        "number_of_replicas" : 1
    }
}'
```

Restoring to a different cluster

To restore a snapshot to a different cluster, you first need to register the repository from where the snapshot needs to be restored to a new cluster.

There are some additional considerations that you need to take in this process:

- The version of the new cluster must be the same or greater than the cluster from which the snapshot had been taken
- Index settings can be applied during snapshot restoration
- The new cluster need not be of the same size (the number of nodes and so on) as the old cluster
- An appropriate disk size and memory must be available for restoration
- The plugins that create additional mapping types must be installed on both the clusters (that is, attachment plugins); otherwise, the index will fail to open due to mapping problems.

Manual backups

Manual backups are simple to understand, but difficult to manage with growing datasets and the number of machines inside the cluster. However, you can still give a thought to creating manual backups in small clusters. The following are the steps needed to be performed to create backups:

- Shut down the node.
- Copy the data to a backup directory. You can either take a backup of all the indices available on a node by navigating to the `path_to_data_directory/cluster_name/nodes/0/` directory and copy the complete indices folder or can take a backup of the individual indices too.
- Start the node.

Manual restoration

Manual restorations also require steps similar to those used when the creating backups:

- Shut down the node
- Copy the data from a backup directory to the indices directory of datapath
- Start the node

Securing Elasticsearch

Elasticsearch does not have any default security mechanisms. Anyone can destroy your entire data collection with just a single command. However, with the increasing demand of securing Elasticsearch clusters, the Elastic team has launched a new product called shield that provides you with a complete security solution including authentication, encryption, role-based access control, IP filtering, field- and document-level security, and audit logging. However, if you cannot afford shield, there are other ways to protect Elasticsearch. One way can be to not expose Elasticsearch publicly and put a firewall in front of it to allow access to only a limited number of IPs. The other way is to wrap Elasticsearch in a reverse proxy to enable access control and SSL encryption. In this chapter, we will see how you can secure your Elasticsearch cluster using a basic HTTP authentication behind a reverse proxy.

In the remaining sections, we will go on to learn how to use Nginx to secure an Elasticsearch cluster. The commands used to set up Nginx and Basic Auth work on Ubuntu 12.04 and above. To set up the same on Centos systems, you can get the installation guide at the following URL:

```
https://gist.github.com/bharvidixit/8b00fdc85f8d31391876
```

Setting up basic HTTP authentication

HTTP authentication allows you to secure Elasticsearch using username- and password-based access. You can do this by installing the `apache-utils` package:

```
sudo apt-get update
sudo apt-get install apache-utils
```

Now, let's create a password file with this command:

```
sudo htpasswd -c /etc/nginx/.htpasswd username
```

The preceding command will prompt you to create a password for the username user, as shown in the following screenshot:

```
New password:
Re-type new password:
Adding password for user username
```

Once you create the password, a file with the `.htpasswd` name will be created inside the `/etc/nginx` directory in the format of `login:password`.

Setting up Nginx

Run the following command to install Nginx on Ubuntu machines:

```
sudo apt-get install nginx
```

You can find the configuration directory of Nginx inside the `/etc/nginx` directory, which looks similar to this:

```
conf.d        koi-utf  mime.types        naxsi.rules       nginx.conf   scgi_params    sites-enabled  win-utf
fastcgi_params  koi-win  naxsi_core.rules  naxsi-ui.conf.1.4.1  proxy_params  sites-available  uwsgi_params
```

Proxy templates are usually created inside the sites-available directory. This can be created with the following command:

```
sudo vi /etc/nginx/sites-available/elastic_proxy
```

Enter the following configuration lines inside this file:

```
server {
    listen 6200;
    server_name es.domainname.com;

    access_log /var/log/nginx/elastic_proxy/access.log;
    error_log /var/log/nginx/elastic_proxy/error.log;

    location / {
        auth_basic "Elasticsearch Authentication";
        auth_basic_user_file /etc/nginx/.htpasswd;

        proxy_pass http://localhost:9200;
        proxy_http_version 1.1;
        proxy_set_header  X-Real-IP  $remote_addr;
        proxy_set_header  X-Forwarded-For $proxy_add_x_forwarded_for;
        proxy_set_header  Host $http_host;
    }
}
```

As you can see, we have configured the Nginx server to listen to port 6200, which is just a custom port number to connect with Elasticsearch. You are no longer required to connect Elasticsearch on its default port 9200 because it is running on localhost. It's also good if you can create a subdomain for your Elasticsearch cluster (es. domainname.com, in this example), which points to the public IP of this server. If you do not have any subdomain, but have a public IP available on this server, you can omit the server_name parameter.

The main things are written inside the location directive, where we have used the HTTP authentication file you had created. Now only those users who have this user name and password can access this Elasticsearch cluster.

When you are done with the configuration of your template, create a symbolic link of the template to make it available inside the /etc/sites-enabled directory that will be finally loaded by Nginx. To do this, run the following command:

```
sudo ln -s /etc/nginx/sites-available/elastic_proxy /etc/nginx/sites-enabled/
```

You also need to create a log directory to store all the access and error logs. You can do it using these commands:

```
sudo mkdir /var/log/nginx/elastic_proxy
```

```
sudo touch /var/log/nginx/elastic_proxy/access.log
sudo touch /var/log/nginx/elastic_proxy/error.log
```

Once done, start the Nginx server with the following command:

```
sudo service nginx start
```

Now, try to access Elasticsearch with this command:

```
curl localhost:6200
```

You will get the following response:

```
<html>
<head><title>401 Authorization Required</title></head>
<body bgcolor="white">
<center><h1>401 Authorization Required</h1></center>
<hr><center>nginx/1.9.2</center>
</body>
</html>
```

This clearly tells you that to access this URL, you need a valid user name and password. So, it can be accessed using the following command:

```
curl username:password@localhost:6200
```

Here, the username and password are the ones you have created in the previous section.

Securing critical access

You know very well that Elasticsearch is based on REST and provides the HTTP endpoints for all the tasks, such as _search, _delete, _update, _stats, _settings, and so on, which essentially works on the HTTP verbs such as GET, PUT, POST, and DELETE.

Nginx is very good for rule-based access by getting the request parameters and putting constraints on the requests. Let's see how you can do this.

Restricting DELETE requests

To keep your data safe by avoiding DELETE requests, you can do the following configurations inside your proxy template:

```
if ($request_method ~ "DELETE") {
          return 403;
            break;
    }
```

Restricting endpoints

To restrict endpoints, such as _shutdown, you can use the following configuration:

```
if ($request_filename ~ _shutdown) {
                return 403;
                break;
        }
```

A final configuration would look like this:

```
server {
    listen 6200;
    server_name es.domainname.com;

    access_log /var/log/nginx/elastic_proxy/access.log;
    error_log /var/log/nginx/elastic_proxy/error.log;

    location / {
        auth_basic "Elasticsearch Authentication";
        auth_basic_user_file /etc/nginx/.htpasswd;

        if ($request_method ~ "DELETE") {
                return 403;
                break;
        }
        if ($request_filename ~ _shutdown) {
                return 403;
                break;
        }

        proxy_pass http://localhost:9200;
        proxy_http_version 1.1;
        proxy_set_header  X-Real-IP  $remote_addr;
        proxy_set_header  X-Forwarded-For $proxy_add_x_forwarded_for;
        proxy_set_header  Host $http_host;
        }
}
```

You can add many other constraints using similar `if` statements as shown in the preceding template. Whenever you edit the template inside /etc/sites-available, it will automatically reflect the changes inside sites-enabled; however, make sure to reload the changed configurations by running this command:

```
sudo service nginx reload
```

Load balancing using Nginx

If you have more than one client node in your Elasticsearch cluster, you can create connections to all of the client nodes for high availability. However, to load balance the requests in addition to cluster security, you can use the power of Nginx.

For example, you have three client nodes with the IP addresses, 192.168.10.42, 192.168.10.43, and 192.168.10.44. The following is a sample configuration that will listen to your proxy server subdomain or the public IP address (can be a private IP if not an Internet-facing ES) and will distribute the load to the Elasticsearch clients in a round-robin fashion:

```
upstream elasticsearch_servers {
    server 192.168.10.42:9200;
    server 192.168.10.43:9200;
    server 192.168.10.44:9200;
}
server {
    listen 6200;
    server_name es.domainname.com;

    access_log /var/log/nginx/elastic_proxy/access.log;
    error_log /var/log/nginx/elastic_proxy/error.log;

    location / {
        auth_basic "Elasticsearch Authentication";
        auth_basic_user_file /etc/nginx/.htpasswd;

        if ($request_method ~ "DELETE") {
                return 403;
                  break;
        }
        if ($request_filename ~ _shutdown) {
                return 403;
                break;
        }

        proxy_pass http://elasticsearch_servers;
        proxy_http_version 1.1;
        proxy_set_header  X-Real-IP  $remote_addr;
        proxy_set_header  X-Forwarded-For $proxy_add_x_forwarded_for;
        proxy_set_header  Host $http_host;
        }
}
```

See the upstream directive in the preceding configuration template that holds all the IP and ports of the Elasticsearch clients using the `elasticsearch_servers` name. The `proxy_pass` directive now contains the name of the upstream directive instead of a single client address.

Nginx also provides options to load balance requests such as least connected, weighted, and session persistence. To use them, you can go through the load balancing guide of Nginx at `http://nginx.org/en/docs/http/load_balancing.html` and utilize them to give more power to your Elasticsearch cluster.

Summary

In this chapter, you learned how to create data backups of an Elasticsearch cluster and restore them back into the same or another cluster. You also learned how to secure Elasticsearch clusters and load balance them using Nginx.

Finally, we have reached the end of the book, and we hope that you have had a pleasant reading experience. Elasticsearch is vast, and covering every tiny detail in this book was not possible. However, as per the goal, it covers almost every "essential" topic of Elasticsearch for developers to start from scratch and to be able to manage and scale an Elasticsearch cluster on their own. Most interestingly, this book serves both Java and Python programmers under one hood.

Not only has Elasticsearch matured, but the community around this technology is also much more mature now. If you face any issue, you can post your questions to the official user discussion group: `https://discuss.elastic.co`.

We also suggest you keep visiting the official blog of Elasticsearch at `https://www.elastic.co/blog` to keep yourself updated with the latest and greatest news around this technology.

With all this knowledge and everything you have learned throughout this book, you are now fully equipped to create and manage a full-blown search and analytics solutions based on Elasticsearch. We wish you the best!

Index

C

function_score query
about 165
decay functions 173, 174
field_value_factor 168, 169
parameters 166
script_score 170-172
weight function 167

G

geo-aggregations 110, 111
geo bounding box query 107
geo distance aggregation
about 111, 112
bounding boxes, using with 113, 114
geo distance query 104, 105
geo distance range query 106
Geohashes
versus Quadtree 117
geo-point data
indexing 102, 103
querying 104
sorting, by distance 109, 110
working with 102
geo-point fields
mapping 102
geo-shape data
indexing 117
querying 118-120
geo-shape fields
mapping 117
geo-shapes
about 114
circle 116
envelope 116
linestring 115
point 115
polygon 116
geo-spatial data 101

H

Hadoop plugins
references 194
has_child query 138, 139
has_parent query 139
Head plugin
installing, for Elasticsearch 12

histogram aggregation
about 89
building 90
response, parsing 90

I

implications 98, 99
index
about 5
analysis options 32
building, with sample documents 163, 164
creating 14
mappings, inserting in 38
settings, modifying during restore 200, 201
indices
renaming 199
Information Based (IB) 162
installation directory layout,
Elasticsearch 8, 9
installing
Elasticsearch, on Centos 8
Elasticsearch, on Ubuntu 7
Elasticsearch plugins 11
elasticsearch-py 43
Head plugin, for Elasticsearch 12
Pip 42
Sense, for Elasticsearch 13
virtualenv 42
inverted indexes 23, 24

J

Java plugins 11
JavaScript Object Notation (JSON) 4
JVM and OS dependencies, of Elasticsearch
reference link 6

K

keyword analyzer 25

L

language analyzer
about 26
reference link 26

Thank you for buying
Elasticsearch Essentials

About Packt Publishing

Packt, pronounced 'packed', published its first book, *Mastering phpMyAdmin for Effective MySQL Management*, in April 2004, and subsequently continued to specialize in publishing highly focused books on specific technologies and solutions.

Our books and publications share the experiences of your fellow IT professionals in adapting and customizing today's systems, applications, and frameworks. Our solution-based books give you the knowledge and power to customize the software and technologies you're using to get the job done. Packt books are more specific and less general than the IT books you have seen in the past. Our unique business model allows us to bring you more focused information, giving you more of what you need to know, and less of what you don't.

Packt is a modern yet unique publishing company that focuses on producing quality, cutting-edge books for communities of developers, administrators, and newbies alike. For more information, please visit our website at www.packtpub.com.

About Packt Open Source

In 2010, Packt launched two new brands, Packt Open Source and Packt Enterprise, in order to continue its focus on specialization. This book is part of the Packt Open Source brand, home to books published on software built around open source licenses, and offering information to anybody from advanced developers to budding web designers. The Open Source brand also runs Packt's Open Source Royalty Scheme, by which Packt gives a royalty to each open source project about whose software a book is sold.

Writing for Packt

We welcome all inquiries from people who are interested in authoring. Book proposals should be sent to author@packtpub.com. If your book idea is still at an early stage and you would like to discuss it first before writing a formal book proposal, then please contact us; one of our commissioning editors will get in touch with you.

We're not just looking for published authors; if you have strong technical skills but no writing experience, our experienced editors can help you develop a writing career, or simply get some additional reward for your expertise.

ElasticSearch Server

ISBN: 978-1-84951-844-4   Paperback: 318 pages

Create a fast, scalable, and flexible search solution with the emerging open source search server, ElasticSearch

1. Learn the basics of ElasticSearch like data indexing, analysis, and dynamic mapping.

2. Query and filter ElasticSearch for more accurate and precise search results.

3. Learn how to monitor and manage ElasticSearch clusters and troubleshoot any problems that arise.

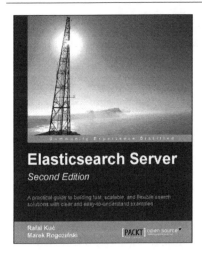

Elasticsearch Server
Second Edition

ISBN: 978-1-78398-052-9   Paperback: 428 pages

A practical guide to building fast, scalable, and flexible search solutions with clear and easy-to-understand examples

1. Learn about the fascinating functionalities of ElasticSearch like data indexing, data analysis, and dynamic mapping.

2. Fine-tune ElasticSearch and understand its metrics using its API and available tools, and see how it behaves in complex searches.

3. A hands-on tutorial that walks you through all the features of ElasticSearch in an easy-to-understand way, with examples that will help you become an expert in no time.

Please check **www.PacktPub.com** for information on our titles

ElasticSearch Cookbook

Second Edition

ISBN: 978-1-78355-483-6   Paperback: 472 pages

Over 130 advanced recipes to search, analyze, deploy, manage, and monitor data effectively with ElasticSearch

1. Deploy and manage simple ElasticSearch nodes as well as complex cluster topologies.

2. Write native plugins to extend the functionalities of ElasticSearch to boost your business.

3. Packed with clear, step-by-step recipes to walk you through the capabilities of ElasticSearch.

Elasticsearch Blueprints

ISBN: 978-1-78398-492-3   Paperback: 192 pages

A practical project-based guide to generating compelling search solutions using the dynamic and powerful features of Elasticsearch

1. Discover the power of Elasticsearch by implementing it in a variety of real-world scenarios such as restaurant and e-commerce search.

2. Discover how the features you see in an average Google search can be achieved using Elasticsearch.

3. Learn how to not only generate accurate search results, but also improve the quality of searches for relevant results.

Please check **www.PacktPub.com** for information on our titles